The Girl's
to New York Nightlife

Cleo Murphy
8 Coffeys Row
Kenmare
Co. Kerry

By Daniella Brodsky

Illustrations by Sujean Rim

HANGOVER MEDIA, NEW YORK

ACKNOWLEDGMENTS

I raise my glass to Chris Hoffman for believing in me, no questions asked; to my editor, for telling it like it is and forcing me to be logical (not a simple task), and for taking the time to find out if, in fact, Derek Jeter really is considered a "hottie;" to all of the bar, spa, salon and shop proprietors, bartenders, and publicists for answering my never-ending list of questions and for making my job lively and enjoyable; to Mike, for his inspiration, feedback, and love; to Neha for once hitting no less than five bars with me in a single evening; to Mimosa for her club expertise and truthful input; to Debora for being there at the start of it all and throughout; to Niki for expressing veritable squeaky-voiced excitement with every phase of this very long process; to Mom for being herself; and to Rye-Rye, who moved on from Blues Clues to Toy Story during the time it took to write this book.

And to all of my friends and family for listening, loving, laughing (and pre-ordering); and especially to Grandma Sylvia for just about everything, and more.

DEDICATION

To all of the people who make up this fabulous city.

In loving memory of my father, who drank only
strawberry daiquiris, but still had a beer belly.

Contents

Clubs 121

Navigate the sea of super-sized clubs, mainstream dance venues and upscale establishments

GIRL STORY #6: **Club Kid 136**
Perhaps our heroine doesn't have what it takes to go clubbing

Land of the Fabulous 140

When you're ready for the glitz, follow the Page-Sixers to these haute haunts

GIRL STORY #7: **Green With Envy 150**
Can just anyone be fabulous?

Eats 156

Satisfy your post-party and morning-after cravings at this eclectic mix of eateries

Beauty Guide 164

For all of your pre-party primping needs—manicures, facials, hair and beyond

Handbags, Heels and In-Between 185

Stock up on looks you'll love and staples you'll need for your evening attire—clothing, handbags, shoes and lingerie, too

Indexes

Introduction*

If you're anything like me, you're ecstatic to receive an invite to the newest so-hot-nobody-knows-about-it-yet boite (and would call in many a favor to get your hands on one), yet you hold your local dive bar in the highest esteem (and treasure those freebies from your favorite bartender). You like to look your best when you head out for the night (even if you've got to hold up the salespeople at Saks a bit past closing time or run in for a 9pm mani/pedi to do so)...most of the time. But you like to reserve the right to say you couldn't care less about impressing anyone, and hit the town in your comfiest denim and college tee, hold the makeup please ...some of the time. And when you go about the task of choosing a bar, there are many factors you consider, which stray from those that men hold dear—such as geography, economy or bartenders with big breasts. Rather, yours is a more complex decision, based on such details as Venus being in or out of your house, your menstrual cycle's current state, the desire to go somewhere chichi to wear a new outfit, or the absolute impossibility of going someplace chichi as a result of one favorite pair of stilettos being at the shoemaker. Then there are the moods: You're feeling old, so you want to go someplace where you can act like a kid again; you're feeling young, so you want to go someplace where you can feel elegant or mature; your girlfriend just broke up with someone so you want a place where she's guaranteed lots of attention; you're hating men, so you want to go somewhere where those ogres wont bother you. And sometimes you want to dance but don't want to commit to a nightclub, or seek chic environs but couldn't deal with a velvet rope brigade. You need a book that understands you and appreciates you and knows how to express his emotions and keep plans and send you flowers, (sorry, got a bit carried away there). Sound familiar?

Enter your fearless author. In lieu of starting a support group to address all of these issues, I thought we should celebrate them. So this book is organized to go along with that non-linear way in which we think. But hey, when you need a quick pick just turn to the back for listings by area or bar type. And it doesn't stop with bar reviews. There's help with all that pre-party stuff too, like a shopping guide, a beauty guide, makeup tricks, hair disaster control, and even dressing tips, all designed to get you out of your apartment or office and onto some fun. There's also a list of late-night dining options to suit anyone's après-party palate. Then there are the stories—all about a girl who has some fun, makes some mistakes, and learns a thing or two—hey, she's probably just like you—lord knows she's like me.

And reading those stories might give you a little bit of insight as to what researching this book was all about. But if you'd like to know a bit more about the process, here's a synopsis: I drank 500 cocktails on evenings followed by 200 days talking on the phone discussing the previous evenings. There were 50 rigorous workouts designed to make up for eating that bagel/pizza/No. 2 meal at McDonald's at four in the morning. I made mad dashes to find something to wear 76 times and returned home empty-handed about 40 times. Therefore, I wore the same outfit (dark jeans, black boots and variations on the black tank) 150 times. I suffered intolerable frizz about 10 times until I purchased my flatiron, after which I spent 30 hours undergoing conditioning treatments and worrying about how many fried hairs were finding their way into the drain. I said "Get a room," 57 times and served as the recipient of that comment 23 times. I met one jerk, one man with questionable gender preferences, one man who I met for a follow-up date I'd prefer not to think about. And I spent countless hours speaking with 26 guys who never called. I have one very large collection of business cards. I am still taking it "one day at a time" with one guy who is married to his job.

But lots of other things happened too. I had a lot of fun, I got to know some girls from my gym as a result of weekly happy hour meetings, caught up with old friends, tried some great new cocktails, danced some calories away (drank some back), made some business contacts, carried on countless conversations about why women in New York are so damned skinny (that blasted Gisele!), watched 85 Yankee games, created inventive excuses for not waiting on lines, and really sharpened my pool game—okay somewhat. And oh, I have suffered my fair portion of hangovers.

The result, I think you'll agree, is an essential reference guide just for you. Cheers!

Happy Hour

What, I ask, is so "happy" about the need to liven up a nine-to-five existence with exorbitant amounts of alcohol? Is it the groups of stockbrokers, daring each other to out-drink their most recent record? Perhaps it's the recurring cycle of hoping to meet someone great, and instead meeting someone sub-par, just to spend the next week wondering why he didn't call. This early-evening tradition is notoriously a time when you learn things about fellow co-workers you'd rather were kept in the dark, and when you yourself may do or say something you oughtn't have. Still, the evidence is clear, New Yorkers live for the after-work bar gathering. And after all is said and done, happy hour is a good way to keep in touch with those commuter pals that won't trek in on the weekends, and a great excuse to blow off the gym—and it does make for interesting water-cooler talk and instant message gossip.

When you think of happy hour, you probably envision a spot with dollar drafts and "Oh What A Night" playing on the jukebox. And while there are many such traditional spots in this city, there are so many out-of-the-box choices, that you can easily vary the locale if not the chain of events. Here's a list of places that will suit whatever mood your weekday may find you in—be it one that clearly requires margarita therapy, the attention of the opposite sex, or even a more targeted mission—like finding yourself a lawyer.

Remember: In a city with so many bars, some find their niche as great after-work spots, but play host to a completely different crowd on weekends. The picks in this section are fantastic for weeknight socializing, so find the section that suits your mood, answer that last e-mail, and enjoy!

MAGNIFICENT MARGARITAS

Is there nothing more sacred than the connection between woman and margarita? Men can keep their dogs; I'll take a margarita—frozen, flavored, or good old-fashioned lime (salted or otherwise)—anytime.

Benny's Burritos

113 Greenwich Ave. (btw. Jane and W. 12th Sts.)

West Village 212-727-3560

Benny's corners the market on creative burritos—purists beware—the curry tortilla may sound odd, but tastes great—as do all of their supersized ingenious frozen drink concoctions. Drink one grande frozen margarita ($9.50-$10.50), in any one of nine flavors, like coconut or kiwi, and you can pretty much write off the rest of the night. In the warm weather, sit outside at the few tables around the restaurant's perimeter. *Cosmos cost $5.50. Open Sun.-Thurs. 11:30am-12am, Fri.-Sat. 11:30am-1am. Happy hour 5pm-7pm means 2 for 1 plain frozen margaritas, Corona and Rolling Rock, late night Sun.-Thurs. (10pm-11pm) enjoy the same specials during Margarita Madness. Sat. and Sun. brunch from 11:30am-4pm add $2.50 to any entrée for a mimosa or tequila sunrise and a bottomless cup of coffee.*

Boca Chica

13 1st Ave. (at 1st St.) East Village 212-473-0108

This Latin American restaurant (which quite unfortunately, does not take reservations), serves fabulous frozen margaritas—traditional, strawberry and guava, as well as pina coladas, passion coladas and strawberry daiquiris ($6.50-$7.75). Put yourself on the waiting list for a table, because the food (like camerones chipotle, $12.50), delightfully flavorful and wallet-friendly, is not to be missed. While you wait—and you will wait—have a drink or two by the ever-bustling bar while munching on fried plantains and yummy black-bean dip—and try to remember that you can't smoke in here. *Cosmos cost $7. Open Mon.-Thurs. 5:30pm-11pm, Fri.-Sat. 5:30pm-12am, Sun. brunch 12pm-4pm and dinner from 4:15pm-11pm.*

Caliente Cab Co.

21 Waverly Pl. (at Greene St.) West Village 212-529-1500

61 7th Ave. (at Bleecker St.) West Village 212-243-8517

Both outposts of this kitschy Mexican eatery promise lots of frosty margarita flavors (that's 12 in all!) and of course, all of the salsa and chips you can eat. While you can opt for a smaller-sized frozen beverage ($7), you might as well do it right and go for the supersized glass (about $13-$15). A favorite on the bridge-and-tunnel (B&T) route, Caliente is always loud and crowded. Bleecker St. Caliente hosts Ladies' Night on Tuesdays with half price select entrees. *Cosmos cost $8. Both locations open Sun.-Thurs. 12pm-2am, Fri.-Sat. 12pm-3am. Appetizers: $5-$16, entrees: about $8-$18. Greene St. location happy hour is Mon.-Sun. 3pm-8pm with half-price drinks. Bleecker St. happy hour is Mon.-Wed. 4pm-8pm for half-price margaritas, well drinks and domestic beers, Sat.-Sun. 3pm-8pm for half price margaritas and domestic beers. This location also offers weekend brunch from 12pm-3pm with 3 drinks ($6.96-$15.95).*

El Rio Grande

160 E. 38th St. (btw. Lex and 3rd Aves.) Midtown 212-867-0922

These frozen drinks (available in 11 flavors $7-$7.50) should come with a warning label: "Do not have more than one!" Just have that first drink and move on—believe me, many an awful hangover has been suffered researching this. And make sure to tell your friends what side to meet you on (Third Ave. or 38th St. entrance) or you may wind up finishing your whole drink, not to mention a basket of nachos (or two, or three), before realizing you've got to take the staff-guided walk through the kitchen to reach your party on the other side. In spring and summer the whole world waits to get inside for a 5 o'clock cocktail—and apparently they let them all in, because it's wall-to-wall twenty and thirty-somethings on weeknights. If you're planning on dinner, you'd better pop over later, after the happy hour crowd thins out, or call to reserve a table. *Cosmos cost $7.50. Open Mon.-Sun. 12pm-12am. Appetizers: $5-$8, entrees: $10-$20.*

Helena's

432 Lafayette St. (below Astor Pl.) East Village 212-677-5151

Stop over on Wednesday evenings for live Flamenco music, or most other nights for DJ-spun merengue and salsa. The margaritas here are the real old-fashioned kind and are available by the glass ($6), or by the pitcher ($20). Don't miss out on terrific tapas at the tables or bar-side. Sip a

"Helenita" (a margarita with a splash of blood orange ; $6 by the glass, $20 for pitchers), or tasty sangria while pondering the meaning of the enormous paper sculpture, which hangs from the ceiling. Cosmos cost $8. Open Mon.-Sun. 5pm-12am (sometimes later on weekends). Tapas: $5-$6, entrees: $9-$11. For tables, reservations are suggested.

Mexican RADIO

19 Cleveland Pl. (btw. Spring and Kenmare Sts.) NoLita 212-343-0140

Dark, cozy and friendly, Mexican RADIO serves up delightful margaritas, made with fresh fruit and an assortment of tequilas. Opt for one of their house concoctions on the rocks (like a Transistor, Code Talker or Short-Wave), a frozen raspberry or lime margarita, or the newest menu addition--a mango and white peach margarita that's not quite frozen and not quite un-frozen ($7-$12). In the bi-level dining room, order up fresh salsa and chips to start and try to settle on just one entrée from their extensive list of options. *Cosmos cost $9 (served in a 12-oz glass). Open Mon.-Thurs. 12pm-11:30pm, Fri.-Sat. 12pm-12am, Sun. 12pm-11pm. Appetizers: $2.95-$8.95, entrees: $8.95-$15.95.*

Rosa Mexicano

1063 1st Ave. (at 58th St.) Midtown East 212-753-7407

61 Columbus Ave. (at 62nd St.) Midtown West 212-977-7700

You must try Rosa Mexicano's signature cocktail, the frozen pomegranate margarita ($8). Year round, the staff squeezes those ruby fruits just for your benefit. Apparently, all that energy, in addition to that which goes into preparing fresh guacamole right at your table, justifies turning a traditionally inexpensive food type into one pricey meal. There's no denying it, the food is great, and the margaritas are first rate, but a meal and drinks can cost close to $70. The place gets extremely crowded, due to its fantastic reputation, so prepare to down a a couple at the bar before your table is ready. *Cosmos cost $7.50. Columbus location serves lunch from 11am-3pm, light menu from 3pm-5pm, and dinner from 5pm-12am. 1st Ave. outpost serves dinner only Mon.-Sun. 5pm-12am. At both locations, the full menu is available at the bar. Appetizers: $6-$12, entrees: $17.50-$28.*

SERENE SCENES

Sometimes an after-work dose of alcohol makes its way to the top of your to-do list as a result of super-stressful weekdays caused by PMS-riddled bosses/"lost" 300-page documents even the Information Technology staff can't recover/broken heel attained by ignoring advice to "stand clear of the moving platform as trains enter and leave the station" at Union Square subway stop. At those times you may want to avoid the loud voices, unwanted advances (of course wanted advances might actually remedy the situation, but you're not looking for attention overload here) and sorority-girl antics and head to more serene environs.

Art Bar

52 8th Ave. (btw. Jane and Horatio Sts.) West Village 212-727-0244

Any bar that plays Billie Holiday and Hole and serves a tasty plate of fried calamari has to be a good enough place to unwind. In the back lounge, mismatched sofas, chairs and coffee tables, a roaring fireplace and art-slathered walls refreshingly bypass minimalist trends and opt instead for a comfy edge, just dark enough so that you wouldn't even know (or care) what time it was. *Cosmos cost $7.50. Bartender's Pick: Yogurt Martini made with Stoli Vanilla, triple sec, pineapple and orange juices ($7.50). Kitchen open Mon.-Sun. 4pm-2am. Food: $5.95-$7.50.*

Botanica

47 Houston St. (btw. Mott & Mulberry Sts.) SoHo 212-343-7251

It's garage-sale chic at this underground bar, compliments of wall-to-wall eclectic furnishings that lend themselves to sitting and staying put. Choose from eight beers on tap and 13 bottles. Happy hour features $3 well drinks and pints from $2-$3.50. *Cosmos cost $5. Bartender's Pick: A shot of John Powers Whiskey ($5).*

Café Noir

32 Grand St. (at Thompson St.) SoHo 212-431-7910

Super Sangria, fantastic frites and intimate tables in an unpretentious environment make this dark, cozy French Mediterranean spot delightful for some quality time with friends. Service is great and comes in adorable male packages! *Cosmos cost $9. Bartender's pick: Mojito made with fresh mint, lime juice, sugar, ice and dark and light Caribbean rum ($9). Kitchen open Mon.-Sun. 12pm-4am. Weekend brunch 12pm-5:30pm. Menu: $3.75-$23.50. Reservations suggested for dinner Wed.-Sat.*

Morgans

237 Madison Avenue (btw. 37th and 38th Sts.) Midtown 212-726-7600

Morgans' brand new facelift sadly means the end of that wonderful communal bar that made flirting so simple. But, there are lots of new reasons to love this below-ground hotel bar. The new interior lends itself to becoming the perfect date spot, with scores of lounging options, like a leather sectional, intimate tables for two, imperial couches and even a lounge-ready Lucite and leather bed. You'll love their new drink list—which truly corners the market in creative cocktails. Another great makeover bonus: an appetizer selection prepared upstairs at Asia de Cuba. Late night, Morgans pumps, with DJ Samantha Ronson spinning Wed.-Sat. But, if the number of celeb-heavy pre-opening soirees serves as any sort of prediction, Morgans may not be as easy to get into as it used to be. *Cosmos cost $15. Bartender's Pick: Twistini made with Smirnoff Citrus, Raspberry and Orange Twist vodkas, sour mix and grenadine ($15). Kitchen open Mon.-Sun. 5pm-12am. Appetizers: $10-$16.*

Red Bench

107 Sullivan St. (Prince & Spring Sts.) SoHo 212-274-9120

This postage-stamp-sized bar, brought to you by the owners of Denizen, doubles as date destination and local hangout. The few tables usually require a wait. Like its sister bar, Red Bench does the flavored cosmo thing; choose from raspberry, peach, vanilla and strawberry. *Cosmos cost $8. Bartender's Pick: Apple Martini ($8).*

PICK-UP SCENES

Some bars are notoriously known as "meat markets." Of course you can meet a man anywhere you go, but if you're a girl on a mission, for whatever reason—be it reassurance of diva status, the breakup blues, a long no-action stint (gosh, we've all been there), or the test run of a new 'do—it helps to streamline the affair by hitting the spots that have a great track record in this category. So here's a list of bars with favorable male to female ratios and fantastic personal success rates.

Bahi

274 3rd Ave. (btw. 21st and 22nd Sts.) Gramercy 212-254-5466

This no-frills boite packs in locals who know that free admission, popular music and cheap drinks add up to a winning formula. Two little back caverns offer a change of atmosphere, if no more space than the packed main room. Super-long lines for the unisex WC make for a series of uncomfortable, yet conversational, queues. *Cosmos cost $7. Bartender's Pick: Stoli Raspberry and Soda ($6). Happy hour Tue.-Sun. 6pm-9pm $1 off all drinks.*

Brother Jimmy's Bait Shack

428 Amsterdam Ave. (btw. 80th and 81 Sts.) Upper West Side 212-501-7515

1485 2nd Avenue (btw. 77th and 78th Sts.) Upper East Side 212-288-0999

1644 3rd Ave. (at 92nd St.)Upper East Side 212-426-2020

All three Brother Jimmy's Bait Shacks are contrived dive-bar replicas, featuring such theme nights as "White Trash Wednesdays," which serve as great places to get in touch with your rowdy side. On weekends, the music's loud, and sardine-packed patrons relish the attitude-free, keg-party mood. There is one element at each Brother Jimmy's outpost that makes it a regular for men—women bartenders with big breasts in cut tee-shirts. And another thing—dollar beers at happy hour. At 2nd Ave. location: *Cosmos cost about $7. Bartender's Pick: Swamp Water—a fruity concoction for one ($6) or in a fish bowl for multiple drinkers (plastic alligator included; $16). Kitchen open Mon.-Wed. 5pm-12pm, Thurs. 12pm-12am, Fri.-Sat. 12pm-1am, Sun. 12pm-11pm,*

Appetizers: $4.95-7.95, entrees: $6.95-16.95. Happy hour specials and food service varies at each location. Call for details.

Heartland Brewery

35 Union Square W. (btw. 16th and 17th Sts.) Flatiron 212-645-3400

If there's one thing that has the power to drag a man from his Sony Playstation, it's beer. And they've got that flowing at this micro-brewery. All the drafts are house recipes, made right on the premises, and surprisingly good. There are five classics available all year round and 25 rotating beers to choose from. The noise level is comparable to that at Yankee Stadium, but the food is decent and a good crowd gathers after work and on the weekends. Outside seating available in the warmer months. *Cosmos cost $7.50. Bartender's Pick: Perfect Margarita made with Cuervo 1800 and Cointreau ($8.50 for a 12 oz. glass). Creative American menu with steaks, burgers, fish — and the bit of everything pu-pu platter is served Mon.-Thurs. until 11pm, and Fri.-Sat. until 12am. Appetizers: $6.95-$15.95, entrees: $10.95-$15.95.*

The Joshua Tree

513 3rd Ave (34th and 35th Sts.) Murray Hill 212-689-0058

Plan trips to this pub/sports bar anytime a serious sporting event is being aired. On weeknights, the number of men in plaid shirts and khakis appears to multiply by the second. This is one of those places you could go to with male friends and still meet someone. If any undesirables happen to come your way, two bars (one up front and one in back) make escaping simple. The small dance space in back tends to be populated by seriously sloshed patrons with two left feet who don't care if they're dancing to Dave Matthews or Olive for the second (or third) time that night. *Cosmos cost $7. Bartender's Pick: Blue Moon Martini made with blue curacao, vodka, pineapple juice ($7.50; more for top shelf). Kitchen open Mon.-Sun. 11am-2pm. Appetizers: $5.95-$8.95, entrees: $7.95-$18.95.*

Lemon

230 Park Avenue South (btw. 18th and 19th Sts.)
Flatiron 212-614-1200

This is a bar that most New Yorkers love to hate. But despite the slurs, it's always packed with men on the lookout. If you do decide to brave it, try a yummy drink concoction like the Memphis or Lexington. If you haven't eaten, grab a table or have a bite at the bar — the American/Asian menu is quite good, as is the service. *Cosmos cost $7. Bartender's Pick: Angel's Kiss made with vodka and Frangelico ($8). Kitchen open Mon.-Sat. 11-12am, snack menu served until 2am Thurs.-Sat. Appetizers: about $10, entrees: about $20. Dinner reservations suggested on the weekends.*

Mad River Bar and Grill

1442 Third Avenue (btw. 81st and 82nd Streets)
Upper East Side 212-988-1832

If aliens landed on earth and this was their first stop, they might very well assume that 1) our population is 95% male; 2) those males (most of whom greatly lack sartorial originality) are driven by two goals — namely, a) to consume as much alcohol as possible in the shortest allowable time span; b) to ogle women. Music falls into the top-forty and dance-favorites categories. The familiarity brings many to the dance floor who might do better to refrain. Mad River airs all major sporting events. From 6pm-9pm Wed.-Fri. drink discounts vary with savings like $3 drafts and $3 bottles. *Cosmos cost $8. Bartender's Pick: Planet Punch made with Myers Dark Rum, orange and pineapple juices, sugar and grenadine ($6). Kitchen open Mon.-Sun. 11am-11pm. Appetizers: $6-$10, entrees: $7-$9.*

Mercury Lounge

493 3rd Ave. (btw. 33rd and 34th Sts.) Murray Hill 212-683-2645

A virtual cookie-cutter of its sister bar, The Joshua Tree, Mercury features comparable testosterone levels and entertainment, via DJ-spun popular tunes Wednesdays through Saturdays, and sports games nightly, on the many televisions throughout the space. Weekends here are jam-packed with locals and B&Ts, but more importantly, plenty of men. *Cosmos cost $7.50. Bartender's Pick: Apple Martini ($8). Kitchen open from 11am-2am Mon.-Fri., Sat.-Sun. 10:30am-2am. Appetizers: $7-$14, entrees: $10-$15.*

Puck Fair

298 Lafayette St. (btw. Houston & Prince Sts.) SoHo 212-431-1200

Named for Ireland's version of Mardi Gras (which gained its moniker from the symbol for male lechery, the billy goat), this bar lives up to all the associations its name conjures. Picture tons of men drinking beer (there are 17 types available), and feasting on traditional Irish fare.(11am-3:30am), and looking for ways to prove their virility. *Cosmos cost $8. Bartender's pick: Irish coffee made with fresh cream, Jameson's or Powers whisky and fresh coffee, served in a heated glass and topped with whipped cream ($7). Stop in for the cheaper day menu before the night shift takes over. Kitchen open Mon.-Sun. from 11am-3:30am. Appetizers: $5-8, entrees: $8-15.*

S&T

3rd Avenue (btw. 38th and 39th Sts.) Murray Hill 212-661-3181

While the crowd at S&T is not normally busting at the seams, whoever's there is normally looking to chat it up. The space is surprisingly large, and done up in the spirit of Disney World meets The Great Outdoors, complete with tree house on the second floor. *Cosmos cost $7. Bartender's Pick: Mandarin Blossom, made with Absolut Mandarin, cranberry juice, orange, Midori $6. Appetizers: $6.95-$9.95, entrees: $9-$16. Kitchen open from Mon.-Sat. 11am-11pm. Bar closed on Sun.*

Sutton Place Restaurant & Bar

1015 2nd Ave. (btw. 53rd and 54th Sts.) Midtown East 212-207-3777

Two floors means twice as much room to pack in the ex-fraternity midtown and Wall Street crowd that find Sutton the perfect after-work spot. And as if that wasn't enough, the gigantic bar has gotten bigger. Nine months out of the year, head up to the heated rooftop lounge, fitted with yet another bar, and big enough to hold 200 patrons of varying blood alcohol levels. There are 21 televisions and four projection screens for game viewing, and Wednesday nights offers a one-man guitar act. *Cosmos cost $9 upstairs ($7 downstairs). Bartender's Pick: Rum and Coke ($6). Kitchen open Mon.-Sun. 12pm-1am. Appetizers: $8-$12, entrees: $10-$16.*

Swift Hibernian Lounge

34 E. 4th St. (btw. The Bowery and Lafayette St.)
NoHo 212-227-9438

Sister bar to Puck Fair, Swift is a great spot to hit when you want a snack, but wish to continue the drinking. Just in case you were wondering, Hibernia was the name used for Ireland back in ancient times, and in keeping with the theme, the head of Irish author Jonathan Swift greets you above the door. The back room is fitted with rustic wooden tables and benches, under oversize chandeliers. The space can get very crowded as the evening progresses—and on weekends it's always packed. Before the night shift takes over the bar you'll save a dollar or two off of the 26 beers served here. *Cosmos cost $8 ($9 for top shelf). Bartender's Pick: 20-oz Guinness (compared to the 16-oz served elsewhere), highly praised as the best around by many an Irish expert ($5). Kitchen open Mon.-Sun. 12pm-4am. Light menu: $5-$8*

Tiki Room

4 West 22nd Street (btw. 5th and 6th Aves.) Flatiron 646-230-1444

It's summer all year-round at this hall of kitsch. Choose from the menu of frosted beverages in all of their island glory, and mourn the vacation you never got to take as you view the tropical scenes on the plasma televisions above the bar. Tiki icons and cardboard tubes-cum-faux-bamboo enhance the Polynesian motif, but the drunk guys sizing you up like you're a frozen beverage in the hot island sun will serve as reminders that you are very much not on vacation, and very much in Manhattan during happy hour. Coming Soon: Sunday night *Sex and The City* viewings. *Cosmos cost $10. Bartender's Pick: Tiki Me Home made with Absolut mandarin, pineapple juice and fresh strawberry purée ($10). Appetizers served Mon.-Sat. 8pm-12pm ($8-$15).*

Turtle Bay

987 2nd Ave. (btw. 52nd and 53rd Sts.) Midtown East 212-223-4224

If you're having trouble deciding between Turtle Bay and Sutton Place (on the same block), you might as well toss a coin because the two are practically interchangeable. Here, you'll find the same abundance of televisions (that's 11 in all), large groups downing shots, and beer (as it was in college) is the drink of choice. In addition to daily DJs, Tuesdays and Wednesdays feature acoustic guitar duos. *Cosmos cost $8. Bartender's Pick: Baby Guinness shot made with Kahlua and Bailey's ($5). Happy hour Mon.-Fri. 5pm-7pm means $3 Bud and Bud Light pints. Kitchen open Mon.-Sun. 11:30am-11pm. Appetizers: $4.95-$7.95, entrees: $9.95-$17.95.*

WHERE THE LAWYERS ARE

Whether you are a lawyer/wannabe lawyer/lawyer-in-training or just want to pick up a lawyer, the word among the esquire crowd is, these are the places to hang.

Bliss Bar & Lounge

256 E. 49th (btw. 2nd and 3rd Aves.) Midtown East 212-644-8750

Dominated by the young working class, Bliss is one of midtown's most popular watering holes. Even with four rooms and two terraces (on the first and second floors) overlooking Sterling Park on 49th Street and 2nd Avenue, Bliss's tables often get booked up by corporate crews. So, if you know you'll be heading over, reserve a table, or even a whole room (depending on the number in your party), at least a week in advance for your group. The neckties (or non-neckties, depending on dress codes) come in droves for a pick-up, a game, and some appetizers too (try the cornmeal crusted calamari for $9). *Cosmos cost $9. Bartender's Pick: Apple Martini made with Skyy Vodka ($9). Kitchen open Mon.-Tue. 4pm-11am, Wed.-Sat. 4pm-1am, closed Sun. Appetizers: $7-$12.*

Divine Bar

244 E. 51st St. (2nd & 3rd Aves.) Midtown East 212-319-9463

There's another British phenomenon hitting our city that New York women will love as much as our beloved Bridget Jones, the wine bar. They're popping up all over, and make for a good choice when you want to feel sophisticated/worldly/romantic/adult. Divine serves 65 international wines by the glass, and sets up the menu by category (like Australian Reds or Sweet Rieslings), for easy picking. If you're looking to broaden your horizons, you can try smaller portions of all of the wines in a category ($7-$28 priced according to quantity and quality). Although this location does not have a liquor bar (downtown Divine does), it does offer 50 beers hailing from around the globe ($5 and up). Upstairs, in the French Boudoir-esque lounge, rich with red velvets, gilt ceilings and flowing curtains, couples, groups of girls and co-workers indulge in an assortment of creative tapas. If you're more into Wall Street men, head to the downtown outpost at 55 Liberty St. (at Wall Street), 212-791-WINE, where the apple martini is made with apple puree for a thicker twist ($12). *Cosmos cost $10. Bartender's Pick: Chalk Hill's Chardonnay ($12.50). Uptown kitchen open 5pm-1:30am. Downtown location kitchen open Mon.-Fri. 12pm-12am. Tapas: $7-$12.*

Dylan Prime

62 Laight St. (at Greenwich St.) TriBeCa 212-334-4783

Leave it to the lawyers to know that carnivorous activity is back. Dylan Prime is a female-friend-ly steakhouse where you can pick and choose your cut of meat and "accessorize" with all of the à la carte sides you want. Top it all off with the sauce of your choice and you're all set. Chicken, fish and vegetarian entrees also available. This restaurant houses two bars — a large lounge opposite the dining room, and a smaller intimate bar inside the dining area. Must-try: 48-oz. martini for four, served on a lazy susan with a ladle, olives and baby fish bowl glass for each drinker ($65). *Cosmos cost $9. Bartender's Pick: Mojito Martini made with mint-infused Bacardi Limon, fresh lime juice and mint, served chilled and straight up ($9). Kitchen open Mon.-Thurs. 6pm-11pm, Fri.-Sat. 6pm-12pm, Sun. 5pm-10pm (closed Sun. July-Sept.). Mon.-Fri 12-2:30 prix fix $20 and à la carte. Appetizers: $6-$16, entrees (a la carte):$20-$32, sides: $6. Reservations suggested at least 24 hours in advance.*

Mercury Bar & Grill

659 9th Ave. (at 42nd St.) Hell's Kitchen 212-262-7755

In Hell's Kitchen, this is the place to go for a stylish scene and a busy happy hour. Mercury has an extensive menu, with well-priced appetizers, like a combo plate with mozzarella sticks, calamari, popcorn shrimp, chicken tenders and crab cakes, and full lunch and dinner offerings. Sit by the bar, or the high tables, or walk to the back lounge. *Cosmos cost $7.50. Bartender's Pick: Deco Special, so special they won't let out the secret recipe, but I'm told its frozen and it's blue and costs $7.50. Kitchen open daily from 11:30am-2am. Appetizers: $5.95-$12, entrees: $6.95-$14.95.*

Pen-Top Bar & Terrace at the Peninsula Hotel

700 5th Ave. (at 55th St.) Midtown 212-956-2888

The type of place the lesser-paid friends will get snippy at the better-paid friends for selecting (think "Friends" episode 205 where the group battles over this very topic), Pen-top mixes and pours 5th Avenue-priced drinks in open-air environs. For those afraid of frizz, heat, or sun — and for the chilly months when going outside is not an option, there's a glass-enclosed portion, which still affords a window to the outside world. If you're looking for light eats, choose from a selection of American tapas like prawns or a cheese plate for two. *Cosmos cost $16. Bartender's Pick: Tiramisu Martini made with Stoli Vanilla, Kalhua, Godiva white chocolate liqueur and a splash of amaretto ($16). Open Mon.-Thurs. 4pm-12am, Fri.-Sat. 4pm-1am. Closed Sun. Tapas: $15-$17.*

Whiskey Park

100 Central Park So. (at 6th Ave.) Midtown 212-307-9222

One of the only Rande Gerber bars not located in a W Hotel, Whiskey Park still has that hot hotel bar je ne sais quoi à la dark woods, candlelight and an I'm-So-Fabulous feel. Whiskey Park also has branches in New Orleans, Chicago, California and Boston, so you can be assured of a safe pick in each destination. The bar serves an extensive collection of single malt scotches and adds new drinks to the menu seasonally. *Cosmos cost $11. Bartender's Pick: Velvet Rope Martini made with Belvedere Vodka, Chambord, sour mix and 7Up ($11). Call 24 hours in advance to reserve a table.*

Also check out these lawyer-popular places, listed elsewhere: Whiskey Blue, Étoile, Bowery Bar, Grand Bar (see index).

Guy checklist

Just because a guy's a looker doesn't mean he's boyfriend potential. But a woman is often willing to overlook some fairly major flaws after one too many single wedding appearances, viewings of *Pretty Woman*, and couple-watching sessions in Central Park. To ensure you haven't gone off the deep end after that second cocktail, just make sure he passes this quick test. You'll want to be certain that all of the following are true. Depending on what time of the month it is and how much you are attracted to him, you've got a leeway of two no's, max.

1. He's moved out of his parents' house. ☐Y ☐N
2. He has most of his hair. ☐Y ☐N
3. He is employed. ☐Y ☐N
4. He doesn't whine about his ex-girlfriend. ☐Y ☐N
5. He knows what Filet Mignon is. ☐Y ☐N
6. He's a college graduate. ☐Y ☐N
7. He has a telephone (cell phones are acceptable). ☐Y ☐N
8. He remembered your name ☐Y ☐N
9. He hasn't been eying other women as they walk by. ☐Y ☐N
10. He's read at least one non-school book—ever. ☐Y ☐N
11. His nose-hairs aren't sticking out. ☐Y ☐N
12. His hobbies include something other than Sega and Alphabetizing his *Simpsons* video library. ☐Y ☐N

13. When he excuses himself to go to the bathroom, he doesn't say, "I gotta take a piss." ☐Y ☐N

14. He doesn't consider Gray's Papaya a gourmet meal. ☐Y ☐N

15. He compliments you on something other than your "physique." ☐Y ☐N

Sometimes you really score and find an uberman who puts the rest of his sex to shame. If he passes these criteria, you've reeled in a winner.

1. He likes to go to the Met. ☐Y ☐N

2. He knows where it is. ☐Y ☐N

3. He volunteers as a Big Brother to underprivileged children. ☐Y ☐N

4. He cooks. ☐Y ☐N

5. He pays for your taxi home. ☐Y ☐N

6. He calls—exactly when he says he will. ☐Y ☐N

NO-FRILLS BARS

Maybe you're having a bad hair day, or you're in just the sort of spirit that prohibits getting all decked out. What you need is a down-to-earth, trend-free environment, where nobody cares if your shoes are from Prada or Payless.

Chumley's

86 Bedford St. (btw. Barrow and Grove Sts.)
West Village 212-675-4449

Choose from 11 signature beers at this former speakeasy—that is, if you can find the door. Chumley's has no sign marking its entrance, so you'd do best to make it your first stop of the evening (read: before you've begun drinking). A rich woodsy aroma dominates courtesy of the bar's long history and the wood-chip lined floor. Chumley's has a heavy dinner menu (lots of pastas, duck, lobster, steak, burgers), and a loyal local clientele. *Cosmos cost $8. Bartender's Pick: Blackberry Hefeweizen ($6). Kitchen open Mon.-Thurs. 5:30pm-11pm, Fri. 5:30pm-12:30am, Sat. 11am-12:30pm, Sun. 11am-11pm. Appetizers: about $8, entrees: $11-$17.*

Doc Holliday's

141 Ave. A (at 9th St.) East Village 212-979-0312

A mix of NYU alum, students, and East Village dwellers convene at Doc Holliday's any night of the week, listening to the country-and-western jukebox croon. Of course, white-trash chic is quite trendy, but Doc Holliday's was around before deconstructed tee-shirts made a comeback. *Cosmos cost $6 (although you might get a funny look if you order one). Bartender's Pick: A shot of John Powers Irish Whiskey ($5.50). Happy Hour means 2 for 1 drinks Mon.-Sun. from 5pm-8pm (Tue. from 2pm-8pm). Come for Mon. Ladies' Night for VERY economical drink specials.*

Ginger Man

11 E. 36th St. (btw. 5th and Madison Aves.) Midtown 212-532-3740

As previously mentioned, beer equals men. At Ginger Man, over 175 international brew varieties are served, so it is not surprising to find numbers of males downing pints on any given evening. This very casual, very large bar makes dressing up unnecessary, but after-work wear will fit in just fine with the suited men who top off their days here. An unexpected bar menu skips the greasy eats in favor of goodies like hot pretzels, shrimp cocktail, salads and gourmet sandwiches. *Cosmos are not served. Limited liquor bar serves classic drinks like gin and tonic. Bartender's Pick: Lindeman's Framboise—a raspberry beer from Belgium served in a champagne flute ($6.50 glass, $9 for pint or bottle). Kitchen open Mon.-Fri. 11:30am-11pm, Sat. 12:30pm-11pm, Sun. 3pm-about 9pm. Food: $2-$20.*

McSorley's

15 E. 7th St. (btw. 2nd and 3rd Aves.) East Village 212-473-9148

One of the oldest bars in the city, McSorley's has been quoted as, "a drinking man's paradise." Well, since 1970, it's really a drinking-woman's paradise, too. That's when they finally "let" us come in. That is, after a Supreme Court order forced them to. Two sorts of homegrown brew are the only beverages available—choose from McSorley light (lager) or dark (porter) ales, with prices that haven't changed much over the years—one beer for $2, or two beers for $3.50. And if you have some pocket change, you can also fill your craving for the most no-frills meals around. Have a sandwich—ham, turkey, liverwurst, tuna or shrimp salad depending on the day— or just $2.75 (cheese optional), or a cheese plate that would make a connoisseur faint—that's American and mild white cheddar (small plate $2; large $3). There is no liquor bar here. *Open Mon.-Sun. 11am-1am.*

Reservoir

70 University Pl. (btw. 10th and 11th Sts.) West Village 212-475-0770

If you're on the lookout for a regular hangout, look no further. From the daily $3 pint specials to the familiar classic rock on the jukebox to the superior waffle fries, Reservoir is home away from home to the exceptionally loyal clientele, who come to play pool, watch the game, lounge in the back or have a chat with the lighthearted bartenders. *Cosmos cost $7. Bartender's Pick: Amstel Light $4. Kitchen open Mon.-Sun. 11:30am-2am. Appetizers: $5.95-$6.95, entrees: $5.95-$12.95. Tuesdays $3 for any pint all day, all night. Sun.-Mon. 20-cent wings after 6pm.*

The Scratcher

209 E. 5th St. (btw. 2nd and 3rd Aves.) East Village 212-477-0030

After "football" (read: soccer) matches, teams come to The Scratcher to brag or complain accordingly. They also come to drink. And apparently to smoke. This wonderful, comfy downstairs bar would be one of the homiest bars in Manhattan if it weren't for the tear-inducing cloud of smoke that hangs over the room. If you do sit at the bar, plenty of props, by way of Irish groceries that decorate the bar back, allow for easy conversation starters. Choose from nine tap beers ($5), and four bottles ($4). Pop in on a weekend for a traditional Irish brunch like bangers and mash from 11:30am-5pm. *Cosmos cost $6. Bartender's Pick: Guinness ($5 a pint). In addition to weekend brunch, kitchen open Mon.-Fri. 11:30am-5pm. Brunch: $4-$10.*

Niagara

112 Ave. A (at 7th St.)   East Village 212-420-9517

Designed with Pizzeria Uno flair, Niagara—tin ceiling, black and white tile floor, long bar and all—makes for a great stop on the weeknight (and weekend) bar crawl. The bartenders are quick and friendly with that "I am actually an actor/singer/guitar player/artist" vibe. Seventies disco and "Oh What a Night" tunes are cranked up to a ridiculous volume. If you happen to make an evening of it, descend the back stairs to the extremely unexpected Tiki bar, where bamboo and palm trees set the scene. *Cosmos cost $6 ($7 for top shelf). Bartender's Pick: Manhattan made with Maker's Mark, sweet vermouth, bitters and a cherry ($7). Happy hour Mon.-Sun. 2pm-8pm offers $2 off all drinks. Tiki bar opens at 8pm daily.*

Old Town Bar

45 E. 18th St. (btw. Broadway and Park Ave.) Flatiron 212-529-6732

Whether or not you're on the lookout for one of the 50-year-old Irishmen who frequent, stop into Old Town from 11am on for a beer and a meal in turn-of-the-century style. The younger after-work crowd gathers here too, for the first-rate comfort food and the come-as-you-are vibe. *Cosmos are $6. Bartender's Pick: Cosmo. Food served Mon.-Sat. 11:30am-11:30pm, Sun. 12pm-10pm. Appetizers: $2-$8, entrees: $6-$10.*

RESTAURANT BARS

Restaurants, boasting requisite-tini lists, happening bar scenes, or premium business district locations, are not just for eating anymore. From the artsy meat packing spots like Fressen to midtown mainstays like Houston's, you can eat and drink, eat then drink, or drink and skip the eating altogether. This list spans culinary categories and price ranges, to keep even the pickiest-palated group planning simple.

Angelo & Maxie's

223 Park Avenue South (at 19th St.) Flatiron 212-220-9200
6th Ave. (at 52nd St.) Midtown 212-459-1222

Steak, steak and more steak is what the spotted cows adorning the walls of this meat-eaters haven indicate. And, if you weren't aware, where there's meat, there're men. After they've spent their company's cash on Filet Mignon, suits head to the back for cigars and cocktails. Learn from my experience: gorging on these oversized portions does not help you to feel desirable. Because tourists flock to this eatery, you never quite know whom you'll run into. *Cosmos cost $7.50. Bartender's Pick: White Chocolate Martini made with Stoli Vanilla, Stoli, Crème de Cocoa, served in a white chocolate rimmed glass ($7.50). At Park Ave. S. outpost kitchen open Mon. 11:30am-11pm, Tue.-Sat. 11:30am-12am, Sun. 5pm-11pm; 52nd St. location closes 1 hour earlier weeknights. Appetizers: $4.75-$12.50, entrees: $10.50-$25.95.*

AZ

21 W. 17th St. (btw. 5th and 6th Aves.) Flatiron 212-691-8888

The Asian-inspired menu is a veritable palate-pleaser; try the trio of tartars appetizers (spicy tuna, salmon and mackerel; $14). Decadent desserts get the splurge-worthy seal of approval ($5-$11). The elegant main floor lounge offers an abbreviated menu in addition to the full dinner lineup. If you'd rather a more intimate meal, take the attendant-operated elevator up to the climate-controlled open-air dining garden. Don't miss the newest additions to the cocktail list: Vanilla Haze made with Argent vodka, vanilla bean and hazelnut liqueur or the AZia Cucumber made with vodka, sake and cucumber (both $10). *Cosmos cost $10. Bartender's Pick: AZ Sparkler made with sparkling wine, lychee puree and fresh lime juice ($10). Lounge open Mon.-Sat.5pm-2am Lounge* *kitchen open Mon.-Wed. 5pm-12am, Thurs.-Sat. 5pm-1am, closed Sun. Restaurant kitchen open for dinner Mon.-Wed. 5:30pm-10pm, Thurs.-Sat. 5:30pm-11:30pm, Sun. 5:30pm-10pm. Lunch served Mon.-Sun. 12pm-2:15pm. Dinner reservations suggested two weeks in advance. Appetizers: $11-$16, entrees: $30-$35.*

Bottino

246 10th Ave. (btw. 24th and 25th Sts.) Chelsea 212-206-6766

What's not to like? Madly good-looking male-dominated staff (one of whom graced the cover of an issue of New York Magazine), excellent Northern Italian food at reasonable prices (like Tuna Tartare $12, Frito Misto — a Tuscan-style tempura $12), attentive bartenders that empty your ashtray almost before you've stubbed out your cigarette and refresh your drinks just as quickly, and a beautiful outdoor space open seasonally. Bottino is a mainstay for the in-the-know set as well as the gallery goers. Don't miss its NoLita sister eatery, Bot (231 Mott St., 646-613-1312), which serves up Tuscan cuisine in a plastic-fantastic futuristic setting. *Cosmos cost $9. Bartender's Pick: Caipirinhas made with fresh lime, sugar, cracked ice and cachaca ($8). Open for lunch Tue.-Fri. 12pm-3:30pm, dinner Mon.-Sun. 6pm-11pm. Appetizers: $5-$14, entrees: $14-$27.*

Commune

12 E. 22nd Street (btw. Park Ave. and Broadway)
Flatiron 212-777-2600

Although Commune doesn't run drink specials for happy hour, its proximity to Park Avenue makes it a disgruntled workers' haven. For $10 you can sip tasty drinks like the Commune Margarita or a Blood Orange Martini. Can't decide on a cocktail? This is a great place to pull a "Can you make me something yummy?" line. Bartenders continuously concoct new mixtures and test-drive them before adding them to the menu. This ultra-chic Flatiron restaurant boasts excellent cuisine and a clientele that apparently hails from the Banana Republic, where button downs and khakis are de rigueur. Park your glass by the communal table up front. Hungry? Walk-ins are almost always accommodated (reservations are taken though). Dinner menu features trendy long-winded imperatives like tuna au poivre with wild mushrooms, hazelnut mashed potatoes and foie gras bordelaise ($27). *Cosmo costs $9. Bartender's Pick: The Radway made with Absolut Currant, Chambord, pineapple and lemon juices and blue Curacao ($9). Lunch served Mon.-Sat. 12pm-5:30pm, dinner Tue.-Sat. 5:30pm-1am, Sun.-Mon. 5:30pm-11pm, Sun. brunch 11am-5pm.*

Cornelia Street Café

29 Cornelia St. (btw. W. 4th and Bleecker Sts.)
West Village 212-989-9319

This rustic candle-lit bistro is Exhibit A of that quaint style that downtown is famous for. Forget attitude. Forget dropping tons of cash. Remember indulging in red meat. Taste the soft bread. And don't skip dessert. Dine alfresco come spring. For a great deal, order a prix fix dinner and split a delightful, affordable bottle of wine. In the downstairs cabaret enjoy jazz, international tunes, and literature readings. *Cosmo costs $8. Bartender's Pick: Sour Apple Martini made with Pucker and vodka, $8. Lunch served Mon.-Sun. 10am-4:30pm, café menu from 4:30pm-5:30pm, Sun.-Thurs. dinner from 5:30pm-10:45pm with café menu until 11:45pm, Fri.-Sat. 5:30pm-12:45am. Appetizers: $5-$9, entrees: $10-$20. Cabaret open 6pm-12am (musical acts go on at 9pm).*

The Globe

373 Park Ave. S. (btw. 26th and 27th Sts.) Flatiron 212-545-8800

If you haven't been to The Globe in a while, you'll be surprised to find the place is now transformed. The formerly bright modern aesthetic is now dark and retro, with details that wink to the 50's, like stainless steel-backed chairs, and white and mirror-blocked walls, mixed in with contemporary accents like dark woods and industrial-inspired lighting. This "American Brasserie" still serves up pretty, pricey eats like tart flambé and risotto. *Cosmos cost $10. Bartender's Pick: Blood orange martini made with Grand Manier, Cointreau, blood orange and fresh lime juices ($12). Open for lunch Mon.-Sun. 12pm-3pm with a bar menu served from 3pm-5:30pm, Dinner served Mon.-Fri. 5:30pm-10:30pm, Sat.-Sun. 5:30pm-11pm. Full menu available at bar and late night menu served Wed.-Fri. until 1am. Appetizers: $7-$12, entrees: $17-$28.*

Houston's

378 Park Ave. So. (btw. 26th and 27th Sts.) Gramercy 212-689-1090

153 E. 54th St. (at 3rd Ave.) Midtown East 212-888-3828

A well-established nationwide chain without the kitschy look associated with the TGIF types, Houston's shoots for understatement with dark woods and sophisticated furnishings in the upper-crust style. Because both outposts are located in business centers, there is no shortage of corporate patrons Monday-Friday. The food is above-par for this class of restaurant, and therefore a bit more costly than you might expect. And you absolutely must try the spinach dip. *Gramercy: Cosmos cost $9. Bartender's pick: Apple Martini made with a recipe so secret, it could not be* *revealed ($9). Full menu available at the bar. Mon.-Wed. 11:30am-11pm, Thurs.-Fri. 11:30am-12am, Sat. 12pm-12am, Sun. 12pm-11pm. Midtown: Cosmos cost $10. Bartender's Pick: French Martini made with vodka, Chambord and pineapple juice ($10). Full menu available at the bar, lounge tables serve appetizers only. Open Mon.-Thurs. 11:30am-11pm, Fri. 11:30am-12am, Sat. 12pm-11pm, Sun. 12pm-10pm. Appetizers $8-$14, entrees: $11-$34)*

Lucky Strike

59 Grand St. (W. Broadway and Wooster St.) SoHo 212-941-0772

Something right out of the Left Bank, stop in for traditional Parisian offerings like steak frites and moules, which you can choose right from the menu painted on the mirrored walls. So, if you didn't get to go to Paris this year, at least you've got a little slice of France right down in SoHo. DJs rotate nightly for an eclectic musical mix. *Cosmos cost $8.50. Bartender's Pick: Vanilla Shanti, a secret sweet and sour concoction ($8.50). Kitchen hours vary, but start at 12pm, and run until at least 2:30am daily. Appetizers: $5.50-$10, entrees: $8.75-$21.*

When the temperature rises, this city sings a different tune. First there's the perennial question of exactly which Shoshanna printed swimsuit will make the must-have list; boots are swapped for flip-flops and strappy sandals, and the task of finding the proper shore house and mates to fill it with begins. And, while the weekend exodus to the Hamptons and the Jersey Shore make for a low-key nightlife scene on Fridays and Saturdays, with available reservations at the most haute restaurants in town, weeknights are an entirely different story. There is something about those mini-vacations (or lack thereof) that makes the workweek seem a perfect time to continue the party. Happy hours Monday-Thursday draw crowds who are in the summer spirit. And what better way to delight in the splendor of summer than to gather at an outdoor spot for an end-of-day drink?

Bowery Bar

40 E. 4th St. (at the Bowery) East Village 212-475-2220

Because of its longstanding hot-spot reputation, B Bar is always booming even if the Hiltons have long gone. The enclosed outdoor garden is one of the largest around. Inside, a retro 50's flair dominates and tons of seating options abound for diners and drinkers alike. The crowd is lively and the drinks are pricey, but Bowery remains a place where a good time can be had by all. *Cosmos cost $10. Bartender's Pick: Strawberry Martini made with Stoli Strawberry, triple sec, garnished with floating strawberry ($10). Kitchen open Mon.-Fri. 11:30am-12am, Sat.-Sun.10:30am-12am. Appetizers: $5-$13, entrees $10-$29. Reservations suggested.*

"Happy Hour/Alfresco" listings continue on page 38.

Party-Girl Pump

Okay, so despite the ritualistic AM resolutions, you didn't make it to the gym for the fourth time this week. You're going out and feeling in less than spectacular shape. When I asked Rich Barretta, from NYC's Duomo Gym, for a quick workout that would produce immediate results, I was sure he would laugh right in my face, but apparently there's some good to be garnered from a last minute sweat session. So, here's his quick pre-party workout that even the most impatient exercisers can benefit from. Don't forget to stretch out before and after. Disclaimer: "Quick" does not in any way indicate "painless."

Bar-Ready Butt: The gluts will feel firm for several hours after this workout. Spend 4-5 minutes doing standard squats, or place your hands on the wall and kick your legs back to your butt, alternating left and then right.

Bye-Bye Beer Belly: Lie face up on your bed (the mattress allows your spine to compress and permits a greater range of motion). Bend knees, clasp your hands behind your head and crunch all the way up, touching elbows to knees. Release halfway down. Repeat at least fifty times. For the next set, crunch up as far as possible and then touch your left elbow to right knee, right elbow to left knee (50-100 reps), twisting from your abs (not from your shoulders).

Cocktail-Ready Cardio: Running energizes and wakes up your entire body. If you have access to a treadmill, finish up with 10 to 12 minutes of high-end cardio interval training (two minutes of running followed by two minutes of walking). To find the right interval heart rate, subtract your age from 220, and take 85% of that number. So, if you're 30, subtract that from 220, which equals 190. 85 percent of that number (161) is the heart rate range you should shoot for during running intervals.

Calorie-Burning Boogie: When you're out, remember that dancing burns 200-500 calories per hour, depending on your intensity. But, of course, one martini contains about 375 calories.

Bryant Park Café

25 W. 40th St. (btw. 5th and 6th Aves.) Midtown 212-840-6500

From April 15th to November 1st, a tent is set up next to the Bryant Park Grill in the park to accommodate the weekend and after-work crowd that wants to act like we don't live in the most overcrowded, under flora'd city in the world. During the week, it's a great big party. The result: a backyard barbecue setup, with the benefit of someone else manning the grill and mixing the frozen drinks. Young professional types whip out their tank tops/khakis (depending on gender) and mingle. *Cosmo costs $7. Bartender's Pick: Frozen Mango Margarita ($8). Open Mon.-Fri. 11:30am-1am, Sat.-Sun. 11:30am-11pm. The outdoor menu offers sandwiches, burgers, salads and quesadillas all under $20.*

Luna Park

1 Union Sq. E. (on the N. side of Union Sq. Park)
Flatiron 212-475-8464

Brought to you by the owners of Ruby Foo's and the Coffee Shop, Luna Park opens in spring to accommodate the outdoor drinking needs of New Yorker's. The food (from pizzas to steaks) is served at umbrella-topped tables or by the bar. You'd be surprised, but the white lights strung around the spot and the foliage beyond can really make you feel like you've escaped the city, that is, until an ex-dot-comer starts telling you about his plans to start law school. *Cosmos cost $9. Bartender's pick: Strawberry Frozen Margarita made with tequila, lime juice, sour mix, a splash of orange juice and strawberry puree ($10). Open May to mid-October, Mon.-Sun. 11:45am-12:30am. Kitchen closes at 11pm for dinner, 11:30pm for appetizers. Appetizers: $6-$12, entrees: $12-$20.*

Union Square Coffee Shop

29 Union Sq. W. (at 16th St.) Flatiron 212-243-7969

In true 50's spirit, Coffee Shop looks like something out of the movie *Pleasantville*. But, they definitely didn't serve up killer Brazilian cocktails like Frozen Batidas in that town (even after the colors popped up). They didn't have so many good-looking men crowded around the bar either. Seasonally, enjoy a drink and some good grub (everything from fresh salads topped with chicken and shrimp to burgers to paella) at the sidewalk tables, but beware that service is notoriously slow, and if the restaurant is busy, everyone at the table has to order something to eat. *Cosmos cost $8. Bartender's Pick: Caipirinha made with Cachaca, ice, sugar and lime ($6). Kitchen open Mon.-Sun. 7am-5am. Appetizers: $6.95-$8.95, entrees: $7.95-$20.*

SPORTS BARS

Hey, girls like sports too. And even if you don't, you're no fool. You know that men do. These spots are ripe with them whenever a big game is on.

Back Page

1472 3rd Ave. (btw. 83rd and 84th Sts.) Upper East Side 212-570-5800

When nothing in the world sounds better than a basket of wings bring a group and your appetite and over-indulge in a plate of 150 chicken wings for $55.95. And heck out the current sporting events o 16 televisions. For big games reservations are a must. During football season, there is a $20 table minimum per person, per game on Sundays. *Cosmos cost $6.50. Bartender's pick: Blue Margarita made with Curacao ($6.50). Kitchen open Mon.-Sun. 12pm-12am. Happy hour Mon.-Fri 5pm-7pm. Complimentary wings, $2 domestic beers, $2.50 well drinks.*

Bailey's Corner Pub

1607 York Ave. (at 85th St.) Upper East Side 212-650-1341

Happy hour here may be more appropriately called "happy day," since drinks specials run from 11am-7pm daily, with rotating bargains. During the day you'll find an older, local clientele. But, after work, and of course on Sundays and Mondays during football season — you'll do well to come as early as you can to grab a seat. With 11 TVs and the NFL package (that means they screen every single football game), Bailey's has a reputation as the go-to for the season. *Cosmos cost $7. Bartender's pick: Black Russian made with Kalhua and vodka ($4).*

Park Avenue Country Club

381 Park Ave. S. (at 27th St.) Flatiron 212-685-3636

This massive sports restaurant/bar is a literal sea of men when important games are aired. And that's probably because they've got 20 TVs, 14 large screens, and even sets in the loo, so you won't miss a thing. Park Avenue offers a martini menu as well as 18 beer selections. Thursdays are most popular for happy hour. Hungry? You'll pay a bit more for food (you've got to make up for all of those televisions somehow), but you've got lots to choose from, like pastas, burgers and steaks. *Cosmos cost $7. Bartender's Pick: Chocolate Martini made with Godiva liqueur and vodka ($6.50). Kitchen open 11:30am-11pm. Reservations suggested for tables during major sporting events at which time there is normally a minimum (about $15 per) person. Appetizers $6-$12.95, entrees: $8-$29. Happy hour Mon.-Fri. 5pm-7pm means 40 percent off most drinks.*

Corporate Cocktails

In my past career, I worked in a corporate setting so stressful that its employees had to convene for happy hour at least once a week in order to maintain a sense of sanity. Ritualistic activity included dishing about the boss (a.k.a. Ms.Queen Bitch), guessing the salaries of co-workers, and commenting on the improper dress of the secretaries. And of course, toasting, with frozen margaritas, the termination of oppressive C.O.Os, C.E.Os and other D.I.C.K.s. This is perhaps the only part of the corporate life I pine for. On one spring day at a bit past noon, I received the following email from a co-worker:

To: dbrodsky@corporationredtape.com
nfethering@corporationredtape.com
pkaplan@corporationredtape.com
From: ksmith@corporationredtape.com
Subj: Bitch Goes Down; Drinks at 6

Ms. Queen Bitch, a.k.a. Tsarina of Hell, a.k.a It's My Job to Make your Life a Living Hell is rumored to be in big trouble, as per Sally Tompkins in H.R., as per the C.O.O's secretary, as per the conversation she overheard in which the "F" word was frequently used in association with Ms. Queen Bitch's name and the word "axe." We are free at last! Frozen Margaritas. The usual spot. 6 p.m. Bring your party hat.

Needless to say, at 4:30, I was so curious and impatient, and feeling rather blimy in my anticipated independence (seeing as the boss would soon be a thing of the past), that I convinced the gang to call it quits early (it was not very difficult), and head over to El Rio Grande before the place got jammed.

By the time we'd finished our first "crack margaritas," as we called them for their intoxicating strength, a number of theories on the rumor had been swapped. There was the "sleeping her way up the corporate ladder" theory, the "finally, they've seen the light" theory, and the "one of us will be promoted and declare a four-day workweek for the whole department" theory. And then I had a "brilliant" idea. It involved a telephone message, profanities, and a list of crimes against nature that Ms. Queen Bitch had committed (numbered from 1-20), which we'd drafted with Christian Dior lipstick on a number of paper napkins.

What happened after that (I was told the next day) placed us in instant crisis mode. Apparently, my "brilliant" idea was shot down by my co-workers a number of times. And after I'd said, "you're absolutely right. That is a ridiculous idea," I'd continue to come up with it once again, as if it was the very first time I'd mentioned it at all. Apparently, this had happened about four times. Apparently, my audience was no longer finding the whole bit as hilarious as I was. Apparently, in my margarita-induced state, I was dead-set on accomplishing this "inge-niatory" (apparently my vocabulary becomes quite creative after a certain amount of alcohol consumption) task. What they didn't realize (I allegedly discovered in the loo) was that I had a cell phone, and that I also knew my boss's telephone number by heart! My talents are being wasted at my "associate" level position, I had been overheard saying on my way outside to place the call on the sly.

I was well through number 17 (asking me to return underwear to Victoria's Secret after 6pm on a Friday) when I heard a noise from my mobile phone. What could that strange beep be, I wondered? Pulling it away from my ear and squinting to look at the tiny screen, I spied a series of numbers. But what could those mean? "I think you have another call," called over a cute guy who had (I'd heard the next day) been intently listening to my monologue, and could barely get the words out, what with the shortness of breath he was experiencing from laughing so loud.

"AND ANOTHER thING ...."

"I knew that, duh," I said, attempting to roll my eyes, but realizing how unsteady that was making me, opted instead for grabbing onto the table nearest me to regain my balance.

I clicked over.

"Where the hell are you?" the voice shrilled.

"Mom?" I asked.

"Um, no it's Monica. You've been gone for half an hour. What are you doing?"

"Oh, I'm just finishing up my message to Ms. Queen Bitch," I boasted my sneaky success.

"You didn't!"

"Uh-huh," I replied.

Ten minutes later (and I'm embarrassed to say, upon completion of a few sick episodes along Third Avenue), we were on damage control. While the sick episodes were in fact unpleasant, they did have somewhat of a sobering effect. It was starting to hit me that I had just left a seriously incriminating Jerry Macguire-on-crack type mission statement on my boss's voicemail that could easily get me fired if the axing rumor turned out to be false.

Creeping into the office, we prayed that Ms. Queen Bitch would be out of the office. Since I had formerly been her assistant, I had possession of her office key and the password to her voicemail. Luckily, the mission was successfully completed. Unluckily, the rumor was untrue, and Ms. Queen Bitch would continue her reign of terror for years to come.

ar Glam

... , e the martini glass feel, but could easily do without the attitude that the most chichi establishments tend to serve up plentifully, head for a beautiful boite that won't jar your nerves with fear of velvet rope burn and inappropriate pocketbook syndrome. Some of these bars are classics that have survived through the trendy phase to become nightlife institutions, while others have gone a bit B&T but are still great for some fun, and still others just have a great ambiance, and that special something that makes them "your place." If you're on the lookout for chic, you've got choices a-plenty, from hotel bars to champagne bars to restaurant bars, and more. These picks have been grouped with your specific needs and expectations in mind to make selection simple.

HOTEL BARS

It's no secret that hotel bars are hot. Just look at the W's, the Mercer, the Hudson, and even little boutique hotels like 60 Thompson to name a few. But, don't overlook the classics that may not hit the trend lists, but offer superior service, chic environs and a great cocktail to boot, like The Terrace at the Stanhope, and the Mark Bar. Hotel bars by definition are places where visitors gather, so mixing with in-the-know city dwellers, you'll find businesspeople here on assignment, or even first-time tourists in puffy painted sweatshirts. Oftentimes the less popular spots are nice and quiet—perfect for a business meeting, or a date.

The Bar at Melrose/The Stanhope Hotel

995 5th Ave. (at 81st St.) Upper West Side 212-288-5800

If you're looking for low-key with superior service and top-notch drinks follow the Met crowd to this old-world lobby bar. Choose a martini drink from Joe's Stanhope Specialties, or even a non-alcoholic concoction, like the Stanhope Summer Tea made with sugar, lemon, grape juice and tropical tea ($5, drinks change seasonally). If you're going for strong, test out the watermelon martini. As free bar buffets go, the one here is delightful, with a selection of olives, craisins and almonds. But if you'd rather a more substantial bite, the full dinner menu from the Melrose restaurant is available until closing. *Cosmos cost $12. Bartender's Pick: The Flirtini made with Ketel One vodka, pineapple juice topped with Mumm's champagne ($10). Open Mon.-Thurs.11:30am-12am, Fri.-Sat. 11:30am-1am.*

Cherry at the Tuscany W Hotel

120 E. 39th St. (btw. Lexington and Park Aves.) Midtown 212-519-8508

You know that red is *the* color this season, but you just can't pull it off. Instead of dressing the part, choose a bar done up in the hot hue. At Cherry, crimson is the color of choice—from leather seats, to the apple-hued pool table, to the walls. Lounge at the tables in front, or follow the stairs down to the back room, where cozy tables line the room's perimeter, beneath black and white prints of celebrities, and a second bar awaits. Cherry is great for weeknight drinks, since the Murray Hill population is young, and apparently thirsty, and it's just provocative enough to provide a not-so-subtle hint to a promising date. *Cosmos cost $11. Bartender's Pick: Apple Martini made with apple pucker, choice of vodka and a splash of sour mix ($11).*

(The Mercer) Kitchen

99 Prince Street (at Mercer St.) SoHo 212-966-5454

If you happen to know someone who's staying at the Mercer Hotel (that's André Balazs' SoHo spot—you may recognize his name from L.A. hotels like the Standard, Chateau Marmont and Sunset Beach), then you can be their guest in the lobby lounge all night, ordering from room service even after the bar closes, while everyone by the bar stares through the glass, wondering if you are that girl from that movie/that ad/that reality television show. Mortals and non-hotel guests can sip cocktails and order light eats from the cocktail menu, like tuna spring roll with soybean puree ($7) and raw tuna wasabi pizza ($6). In the surprisingly large downstairs dining room, Jean Georges Vongerichten (of Jean George, Vong and Jojo's) prepares American/French/Asian cuisine. Reservations are suggested for the restaurant. *Cosmos cost $10. Bartender's Top Pick: The Red Butterfly—fresh muddled raspberries, simple syrup (sugar water), fresh lime juice, and champagne, with raspberry garnish ($15). The appetizer menu is served Mon.-Sat 6pm-12am, Sun. 6pm-11pm. on Sun. The bar stays open an hour after the restaurant closes. Restaurant open Mon.-Thurs. 6pm-12am, Fri. and Sat. 6pm-1am, Sun. 6pm-11pm. Appetizers: $9-$14, entrees: $19-$30.*

Olives

201 Park Ave. So. (at 17th St.) Flatiron 212-353-8345

WARNING: YOU CANNOT SMOKE HERE. What do they think this is, L.A.? Well-lit and a bit too crowded at happy hour and on weekends, Olives sports the same minimalist décor as the other W hangouts, but with a much more traditional hotel-like feel. Bookshelves line the walls, and chess and tick-tack-toe boards are stocked in the lounge. The Olives menu is inspired by the cuisines of Italy, France and Spain, where those savory little delights hail from. *Comsos cost $12. Bartender's Pick: Apple Martini ($12). Kitchen open Mon.-Wed. 7am-10:30am for breakfast, 12pm-2:30pm for lunch, 5:30pm-10pm for dinner; Thurs. same schedule all day, but last reservation taken for 10pm; Fri-Sat. after breakfast, brunch served from 10am-2pm; last reservation at 11pm; Sun. brunch hours and last dinner reservation at 9:30pm. Lounge menu available until bar closes. Appetizers: $8-$12, entrees: $18-32.*

Underbar/At the W Hotel

201 Park Ave. So. (at 17th St.) Flatiron 212-358-1560

It appears that Randy Gerber has truly outdone himself on this one. Glide past the velvet rope (with no attitude on a Friday night!) and descend the staircase, lit by flickering red votive candles and notice the sweet incense in the air. If you're wearing a coat you will be asked (translation: required) to check it. But, the reason is clear — there are so many people mingling in Underbar you'll be hard-tested to make it from one side of the room to the other. There are plenty of lounging options upon which to rest your teetering-heeled feet and scan the room for obvious pursuits. But, if you're up for a more private affair, phone ahead to reserve a seat at one of the curtained-off nooks at the room's perimeter. Tables can accommodate up to 13 people. *Cosmos cost $11. Bartender's Pick: Apple Martini ($11).*

Wet Bar/At the W Hotel

130 Lexington Ave. (btw. 38th and 39th Sts.)

Midtown East 212-592-8844

Rande Gerber makes bars into legends, which is exactly what Wet Bar is, although it's spiraled down from celeb haunt to bridge-and-tunnel status over the years. Reds, velvet, leather and scantily clad waitresses still make for a provocative scene where cosmos are the drink of choice and turtle necks have made their biggest comeback ever. *Cosmos cost $11. Bartender's Pick: Apple Martini made with vodka, apple pucker, and a splash of sour mix, garnished with a wedge of granny smith apple ($12).*

Whiskey Blue/W New York Hotel

541 Lexington Ave. (btw. 49th and 50th Sts.)

Midtown East 212-755-1200

W, W, W — Here I go again. Reserve visits here for out-of-towners who've heard the name, but have yet to have the W experience. The brightly-lit glass façade makes you feel like you're out doors, or at least on display — which you are. A huge red velvet bed stands right in the middle of the space. How's that for an underlying theme? Remember, this W for those nights when you would like to brush up on your flirting skills. *Cosmos cost $11 (made with Skyy Citrus and Cointreau). Bartender's Pick: French Martini made with belvedere vodka, pineapple juice and Chambord ($11).*

BUBBLY BARS

Champagne dreams? Page-Sixers are not the only ones who get to drink bubbly with straws from adorable quarter-size bottles.

Bubble Lounge

228 W. Broadway (btw. N. Moore and Franklin Sts.)
TriBeCa 212-431-3433

What, dare I ask, can satiate the desire for all things beautiful better than a flute of Dom Perrignon and a bit of Beluga? Apparently, many a New Yorker would agree, which is why Bubble Lounge, after five years, still garners a line on weekends. Looking like they've popped straight from the pages of Hamptons magazine, bubbly-craving clients have over 300 bottles to choose from, and 35 champagnes are served by the glass. Can't find a seat by the bar? Head down to the below-ground cavern, where a second bar will satisfy your craving for the bubbly stuff. If you'd like to expand your champagne expertise, try a tasting flight at $25, $50 or $70. *Cosmos costs $9. Bartender's Pick: A glass of champagne, of course! (tasting size $6-$12, full-size $10-$35). Kitchen open Mon.-Fri. 5pm-1am, Sat. 5pm-2am, closed Sundays. Appetizers: $6-$310 (for 125 grams of Beluga).*

Flute

40 E. 20th St. (btw. Broadway and Park Ave. S.)
Gramercy 212-529-7870
and 205 W. 54th St. (btw. Broadway and 7th Ave.)
Midtown West 212-265-5169

Flute sells all three mini champagnes: POP made by Pommery ($14), Piper Brut—Baby Piper ($15), and Moet and Chandon's Mini Moet ($16). True to the name, Flute is a champagne/wine bar (although it also has a fully-stocked bar), offering 100 types of French champagne by the bottle, and 20 by the glass. Fifteen international wines are on the list. The quarter-life-crisis crowd piles in on Fridays, Saturdays and Sundays, drinking and eating appetizers from the French-Vietnamese selection--like spring rolls and smoked salmon--prepared by executive chef Tom Kukoly. DJs rotate nightly and play anything from French lounge music to soul. The tables seat up to 100 in the Flatiron location (reservations are suggested), which is three times the size of the uptown venue. But, if you're one of the lucky 75 key card-holders (or friend of), you can swipe your card through a separate entrance and enjoy a private party downstairs at Club Piper (designed by Jonathan Adler). *Cosmos cost $9, Champartini—Ketel One Vodka, a splash of Chambord, a splash of triple sec, a splash of lime juice mixed and poured into martini glass rimmed with sugar, with 3 oz. of champagne ($14). Appetizers: 5pm-4am. In summer champagne happy hour Mon.-Fri. 5pm-6pm at 20th St.—buy one, get one free.*

49

Morning-After Ritual #1: Shopping NoLita

Heaven knows, shopping is one of the most widely acclaimed panaceas around. Target your expedition to one heavily shop-populated district to make the most of your day. (Re)discover NoLita. If you've not yet visited the designer boutiques just North of Little Italy (that's Spring St. to E. Houston, btw. Broadway and the Bowery), you've done yourself a large disservice. The best time to visit is at the changing of seasons when unique digs bear drastically reduced price tags. Don't miss: A Détacher for unique asymmetrical looks; Calypso for Caribbean style duds; Shoe for handmade shoes from around the globe; Red Wong for clothing and accessories from a mix of designers, Final Home (a project of Issey Miyake's) sells Kosuke Tsumura's unisex tee-shirts, pants and jackets—in a distinctly urban look; shop (or discreetly drool over) uber-designer wares at Language and check out the newest edition of *Visionaire*; ultra-feminine looks in crisp colors line the racks of Tracy Feith (be mindful of the trapdoor); fashionistas with a keen eye for deconstructed tees and equally edgy skirts and pants shop Wang for unique, modern designs; Resurrection's impeccable collection of major label vintage is a must on the shopping tour; pick up those sought-after Cosabella thongs and a unique ensemble to boot at Hedra Prue; have a team of experts fit you for the best swimsuit you've ever purchased at Malia Mills (you will never buy another brand again).

BARS WITH GLOBAL APPEAL

New York is a rich melting pot for international cultures. Reap the bene-
fits of this diversity by filling your glass with everything from Soviet treats
to French indulgences.

Lava Gina

116 Avenue C (btw. 7th and 8th Sts.) East Village 212-477-9319

How can you not love a bar named for "a hot girl named Gina?" Somewhat new to the East Village,
it's got the whole world in its hands, or so you might guess, from the international wine list (spanning California, Spain, South Africa, Argentina and France), world music spun nightly, and even
their answer to the standard cosmopolitan—the Lava Gina ($9), jazzed up with a bit of bissap,
an elixer from a West African flower. Tapas served all night. And belly dancers and astrologers
make for mystic Thursdays. *Cosmos costs $9. Bartender's Pick: Apple Lavatini made with Absolut
Currant or Mandarin, apple pucker, Blue Curacao ($9). Tapas: $5-$7.*

Pravda

281 Lafayette St. (btw. Prince and Houston Sts.) SoHo 212-226-4696

Once the cool kingpins discover that civilians (easily detected by last season's duds or lack of
newest LV purse incarnation) have infiltrated their latest haunt, it's time to move on to the next
spot. It's been some time since Pravda's coup d'état, but that hasn't hurt business for the Russian
wonderland. Apparently, now you don't have to wear the newest low-slung/high-slung/corseted
belt to appreciate caviar and blinis and an authentic martini. And the best part about the new
regime? You can actually get inside (self-esteem intact). It's still best to make a reservation if
you'd like a table, no waiting, thank-you. And from 5:30 (opening time) until 6:30 all tables
receive a complementary platter of savories, like cheese sticks, olives and smoked trout. *Cosmos
coss $10. Bartender's Pick: Leninade made with citrus vodka, lemon juice, simple syrup, mint and
grenadine ($10; more for top shelf vodkas). Kitchen open Fri.-Sat. 5:30pm-4am, Mon.-Thurs.
5:30pm-2:30pm. Appetizers: $5-$11, entrees: $12-$16, caviar: $15-$20.*

Villard/At the New York Palace Hotel

455 Madison Ave. (at 50th St.) Midtown 212-303-7757

Anyone who's anyone has a favorite hotel bar these days. Dahhling everyone does the W's. Morgans is great for romance. The Grands (SoHo and TriBeCa) are a perfect mainstay. But when you want to surprise, you'll have to be a bit more original. In a so-overdone-it's-actually-cool Louis the XIV theme, fitted with more gilded frames, velvets, gilt chandeliers and Versace china than one could ever want, much less need to see in a lifetime, Villard's effect is a bit of levity that makes snobbery impossible. But you won't find any French fries or French dressing on the menu. With high drink prices and decadent appetizers like foie gras at sub-fabulous quality, you'll never have to actually go to Paris at all. Sit in ornate seating arrangements in one of the four rooms, practice phrases like, "But of course," and "I could just die," and just don't take it too seriously. Your group will never forget it, that's for sure. *Cosmos cost $13. Bartender's Pick: Redentore made with fresh pineapple juice, a splash of rum and chilled champagne ($12). Kitchen hours: Mon.-Sat. 5pm-10:30pm. Appetizers: $16-$25.*

DINNER WITH FRIENDS

What better way to spend an evening than enjoying a great meal and a round of drinks with the ladies in posh environs? It's your time to reminisce, boy-bash, share beauty secrets, complain about those five pounds you just can't lose, or gush about that new promotion. Whether it's a birthday celebration, the kick-off of a bachelorette party, a holiday feast or just a simple gathering, your group of gals will be glad you've picked one of these restaurants. And as the planner, you'll save yourself a lot of work—since the bar scene at each of these eateries is just as good as the food. Consider it one-stop-shopping. If only everything in life was this simple…

Aleutia

220 Park Ave. So. (at 18th St.) Flatiron 212-529-3111

This relatively new Asian-inspired restaurant/lounge incorporates minimalist, retro furnishings with elaborately elegant floral arrangements, in a loft-like space accented with cool stainless steel. The locals and Park Avenue corporate types have taken to Aleutia with a vengeance. It's busy. Elbows are rubbing. Deals are being made. I-love-you's are being exchanged. Sushi and decadent desserts are being savored. Dinner reservations are suggested on Wednesdays (apparently the day people want to celebrate getting through half the work week) and Saturdays (when people want to mourn the end of the weekend and the beginning of the next work week). Every night, the dining rooms (on the second level and at the rear of the main floor) offer a prix fixe sushi/seafood-heavy menu. At the bar and lounge order any item à la carte, or select from the light bites on the "tastes and teasers" menu ($10-$15). *Cosmos cost $9/Blood Orange Cosmo (Stoli Orange, triple sec, lime juice, blood orange juice and a splash of cranberry juice) $10. Bartender's pick: The Aleutian Iced Tea: Stoli Orange infused with Hawaiian tea, a splash of passionfruit, mint infused simple syrup and water ($10). Dinner served Mon.-Wed. 5:30pm-11pm, Thurs.-Sat. 5:30pm-11:30pm. Tastes and teasers available until closing (2am) nightly. Prix fixe: 3 courses for $42, 4 courses $45, 5 courses $55 per person.*

Asia de Cuba

237 Madison Ave. (btw. 37th and 38th Sts.)

Midtown East 212-726-7755

An oldie, but a goodie, Asia de Cuba is home to the best dessert in New York City, the Latin Lover, a flourless chocolate cake layered with chocolate mousse, doused with white chocolate anglaise and garnished with a white chocolate bar ($9); then there's the Tiki-Puka-Puka ($25), a communal drink that makes everyone at your table look stupid drinking from an oversized bowl with large bendy straws. Upstairs, the elegant lounge area overlooks a delightfully soothing waterfall. Reserve a seat at the communal table on the main floor—it's a great way to mingle. *Cosmos cost $10. Bartender's Pick: Mambo King made with Stoli Raspberry and champagne, served in a champagne glass ($14). Kitchen open Mon.-Wed 12pm-11pm (last reservation), Thurs.-Fri. 12pm-12:30am, Sat. 5:30pm-12:30am, Sun. 5:30pm-11pm. Appetizers: $15-$25, entrees: $22-$60 (all plates meant for sharing).*

Cafeteria

119 7th Ave. (at 17th St.) Chelsea 212-414-1717

For those times when meeting men who play for your team is not the goal, Cafeteria is a great choice for yummy food (like fried chicken and waffles—yes, waffles and cobb salads). Stop into the downstairs lounge on a Sunday from 8pm-2am, when the DJ is grooving and the $5 cosmos sale is on. The ultra-modern stainless steel and white interior lends Cafeteria a hipster feel (a Chelsea necessity), and the open-front and outdoor seating make it a perfect spring/summer haunt. But, the real sell is that the kitchen is open 24 hours a day (bar opens at noon on Sundays, 8am all other days). In the downstairs lounge smoking is permitted and the full menu is served from 6:30pm-4am nightly. *Cosmos cost $8. Bartenders Pick: Cafeteria Cosmo made with passionfruit ($9). Also see Eats, page 157.*

Five Points

31 Great Jones St. (btw. Lafayette St. and the Bowery) East Village 212-253-5700

Like a quaint New England restaurant, Five Points provides comfort in the form of creative American cuisine, a variety of cozy cocktails and an extensive assortment of teas. Comfort, though, does come at a price. Expect a large tab. *Cosmos cost $8. Bartender's Pick: Blackberry Bailey's Spritzer made with champagne and fresh blackberry juice infused with Bailey's ($8). Kitchen open Mon.-Sun. 6pm-12am, and for Sun. brunch 11:30am-3pm. Appetizers: $6-$10, entrees: $17-$27.*

Global 33

99 2nd Ave. (btw. 5th and 6th Sts.) East Village 212-477-8427

Returning from the ashes, after a fire destroyed its former location (right down the block), Global 33 is back, with a short, yet creative tapas menu and a strong sangria to boot. You must try the lobster quesadilla. Top it off with a flourless chocolate espresso torte. The airplane theme is played out nicely in a thoroughly modern fashion, and the long, narrow space fills up on the weekends. While the bar area is small, the locals and trendmeisters manage to find room. *Cosmos cost $7. Bartender's Pick: Global Gimlet made with Skyy vodka, fresh-squeezed lime juice, simple syrup ($8). Kitchen open Mon.-Thurs. 6pm-12am, Fri.-Sat. 6pm-12:30am, Sun. 11am-12am. Tapas: $7-$13. Reservations recommended on weekends.*

Markt

401 W. 14th St. (at 9th Ave.) West Village 212-727-3314

Order up a Lefe, or one of the other 33 beers at Markt to accompany your seafood-dominated Belgian fare. This large, open space is brimming with intimate tables alongside a super-sized bar where beautiful people gather. Forget your diet though — Belgian food is big on frites and mayo. *Cosmos cost $8. Bartender's Pick: Hoegaarden white beer ($5). Kitchen open Mon.-Sun. 11:30am-4:30pm; 5:30pm-1am. Appetizers: $6.50-$13, entrees: $13-$26.*

Park Avalon

225 Park Ave. S. (btw. 18th and 19th Sts.) Flatiron 212-533-2500

The same proprietors that bring us Blue Water Grill, Aqua Grill and other popular restaurants serve up creative American cuisine here nightly. An array of flickering, melted-every-which-way candles could set a romantic tone at Park Avalon, but the noisy scene at the front bar discourages the desire to cuddle. The windowed façade allows the crowd to look across at the joints like Union Bar and Lemon that insure Park Ave. S. is populated with happy inebriates almost every night of the week. *Cosmos cost $8.50. Bartender's Pick: Watermelon Martini made with fresh watermelon juice, Skyy vodka, triple sec and watermelon balls ($8.50). Kitchen open Mon.-Thurs. 11:30am-12:30am, Fri.-Sat. 11:30am-1am, Sun. 11am-12:30pm. Appetizers: $7.50-$8.95, entrees: $10.50-$22.95.*

Sushi Samba

245 Park Ave. S. (btw. 19th and 29th Sts.) Flatiron 212-475-9377

Sushi Samba 7

87 7th Ave S. (btw. Christopher and Bleecker Sts.)
West Village 212-691-7885

When you've tired of the ubiquitous spicy tuna roll, head to Sushi Samba for sushi with a cool South American twist. Colorful interior matched with excellent service and truly unique fare (exibit A: El topo roll made with fresh salmon, shiso leaf, jalapeno, mozzerella, crispy onions and spicy sauce), has made Sushi Samba an instant favorite. The Park Avenue South location is never without a line of folks outside waiting for their salmon seviche. That outpost houses a small bar in back. The bi-level West Village branch hosts a rooftop party seasonally with occasional with DJ and Samba band appearances; come here for Sunday brunch and live music *(12pm-5pm). Cosmos cost $8. Bartender's Pick: Mojito made with muddled mint, sugar and rum ($8). Kitchen open Mon.-Wed. 12pm-1am, Thurs.-Sat. 12pm-2am, Sun. 12pm-12am. Appetizers range from $8-$14, entrees $17-$24.*

Tja!

301 Church St. (at Lispenard St.) TriBeCa 212-226-8900

Grab a seat by the bar and observe the arcane art of making fresh mojitos. Chock-full of pulverized peppermint sprigs, they look, smell and taste like heaven. These are just about the best versions of the South American beverage you'll find in the city. Tja! Has a beautiful understated décor, with high ceilings, lounge nooks and a full dining room. Even the WC displays a noteworthy touch of zen, complete with a river stone-lined sink and natural linen-covered walls. Around midnight the bar area gets crowded with model-types, out-of-towners and your average Joes — all of whom dress in black. The menu is "Scandinasian" (that's Scandinavian/Asian fusion) with reasonable prices . If you can't catch a table, the full menu is available at the bar. *Cosmos cost $10 and are made with O.P. Aquavit (a flavored Scandinavian vodka). Bartender's Pick: Swedish Erotica: Absolut citron, peach and strawberry fruit, served with crushed ice and champagne ($11) Kitchen open Mon.-Thurs. 12pm-12am, Fri.-Sat. 12pm-1am. Appetizers: $8-$12, entrees: $17-$26.*

CHAIR DANCER'S DELIGHT

While many get frustrated with spots that play great music but don't allow you to boogie down, others are actually relieved at not being called to the dance floor. But, if the spirit overcomes you, you can always do a bit of shimmying and shoulder rolling right in your seat at these well-tuned bars.

China White

143 Madison Ave. (btw. 31st and 32nd Sts.) Murray Hill 212-684-0004

Okay, so you've convinced your uptown pals to migrate south of 50th Street. But, they just won't commit to the Lower East Side or the Village. Don't fret — you have options other than the W's and Morgans. China White is a no-attitude spot that plays hip-hop and retro dance music (albeit a bit too loudly) and serves up delicious martini drinks like a chocolate mint ice cream martini at equally pleasing prices (all specialty drinks $9). Staff is super-friendly and will pass your denim-clad male friends through the velvet rope (probably with a warning against repeating the faux pas the next time). Grab a seat at an oversized booth and sit until the bulk of the crowd heads to Joshua Tree. *Cosmos cost $9. Bartender's Pick: China White with Bailey's, Godiva White, and a splash of Chambord ($9).*

Climate Eight

366 8th Avenue (at 28th St.) Chelsea 212-279-8605

This Chelsea newcomer features DJs spinning reggae, soul, R&B and hip-hop on Saturdays. But its lack of a cabaret license means you can't get down to the rhythm in that all-out John Travolta manner. The dark, eclectic décor is graced with all sorts of paintings from rotating artists, massive fish tanks and spacey silver lanterns up above. And refreshingly, you won't be met with attitude at the door. Climate Eight should prove a well-needed addition to the area. *Cosmos cost $9. Bartender's Pick: Climate Eight Ball made with vodka, Red Bull and blue Powerade ($8).*

Nativa

5 E. 19th St. (btw. 5th Ave. and Broadway) Flatiron 212-420-8636

The double-decker space has all the makings of a mini-club, minus the dance floor. It is a shame, too, because retro hip-hop and R&B from the likes of Notorious B.I.G. and (the now notorious) P. Daddy and of-the-minute beats have even the whitest-of-the-white boys chair dancing. On the lower level, tiny tables line the space. Munch on light Asian-style bites from $8-$13. Upstairs, a dark club-like scene seems like more of a pick-up place. *Cosmos cost $10. Bartender's Pick: Apple Martini ($10). Appetizers served from 6pm-12am. Food: $8-$13.*

Parlay

206 Ave. A (btw. 12th and 13th Sts.) East Village 212-228-6231

This is a late night hip-hop hangout. Mod and sleek, thanks to Space Age furniture and seed-like lighting fixtures, Parlay lends itself to lounging about and grooving sofa-style. *Cosmos cost $9. Bartender's Pick: Sour apple martini ($9). Cover $5 on weekends.*

DATE SPOTS

When it's date night, nothing's going to stand in the way of creating the perfect set-up. Nails done—check; hair—check; new outfit of the revealing-yet-not-cheap variety—check. But where, oh, where are you to go? These spots (of varying degrees of romantic) are quiet enough to allow for intimate conversation, and pretty enough to set the mood you're after. What you do once you're there is up to you.

Aubette

119 E. 27th St. (Park and Lexington Aves.) Flatiron 212-686-5500

The space, long and loft-like, is beautifully appointed in the modern, swank manner of many Manhattan bars. To help in your seduction scene, grab a seat by the fireplace. Unlike most other Park South watering holes, Aubette is intimate, and wouldn't be classified as a pick-up scene. The drinks are great, the staff is pleasant, and the appetizer menu is extensive. *Cosmos cost $10. Bartender's Pick: Apple Martini ($10). Appetizers: $10-$12.*

Chèz Es Saada

42 E. 1st St. (btw. 1st and 2nd Aves.) East Village 212-777-5617

Rose petals sprinkled upon the brick spiral staircase in this Morocco away from Morocco are enough to make you feel glam and ready for love. The French Moroccan menu offers up treats like Briouats (that's spinach, goat cheese and onion-filled pastries) for an appetizer, and Lamb Tajine (a traditional Moroccan dish prepared with green lentils and fava beans) for dinner. But, ladies, you'd better make this a diet-free meal, because there's no use in counting up the Weight Watchers points in decadent offerings like Cardamon-scented chocolate cake with pistachio ice cream (desserts are $8). The full menu is available at the bar, along with an extensive French-American wine list that has garnered the Wine Spectator Award of Excellence for three years running. This place reeks of romance. *Cosmos cost $9. Bartender's Pick: The Oasis Stoli made with raspberry purée, cassis, fresh lemon juice and champagne ($10). Kitchen open Thurs.-Sat. 6pm-1am, Sun.-Wed. 6pm-12am. Bar hours: Sun.-Wed. until 1am, Thurs. until 1:30am, Fri.-Sat. until 3 am. Appetizers: $9-$13, entrees $19-$25.*

Reclaim Your Closet (and your sanity)

You know the scenario. All of the clothes in your closet are strewn across your apartment. Nothing looks right. Even that perfect little black dress seems to have turned on you. It's time to face facts. You've got to put an end to last-minute dress stress. Sartorial expert Emily Cho, Image Consultant and Personal Shopper, tells how to do it.

Closet Rehab Rule #1: Prune

If your closet is exploding, a bit of pruning is in order. Take out all of the pieces that fit into the "I'll wear this when I lose five pounds" category and store them in a box. This way, you won't waste time attempting such MacGyver-ish moves as lying on the floor and trying to zip up your Levi's with a coat hanger, you won't be tempted to buy tops to wear with them, and you won't keep fingering them thinking, "I really want to wear these tonight." When you do lose the weight you can put them back in your closet. If, on the other hand, you're holding onto clothing that's too large, have the pieces altered so that you can actually wear them.

Closet Rehab Rule #2: Reorganize

Hang tops with skirts or pants that look great together. To realistically determine if they actually do "look great," try outfits on when your hair and makeup is perfect, and consider accessories and shoes, too. Once you've decided on the smartest combos, hang them in garment bags together, so that you get to know the pieces as an ensemble.

Closet Rehab Rule #3: Allow for Mood Changes

One night you're raring and ready to go, the next you'd give your best Choos to be the invisible woman. Make sure your wardrobe contains a variety of looks and styles so that you don't have to play the sexy/youthful/sophisticated part when you're not up to it. When all else fails, refer to the rule of black—it's the perfect choice for when you're not feeling or looking your best.

Closet Rehab Rule #4: Stock the Basics

Make sure you've got several different types of stockings, bras and panties. You'd hate to pull on that hot new little black dress only to discover you've got an incurable case of visible panty lines. Have lots of accessories like belts, necklaces and scarves, on hand that can add whatever you feel is missing from your get-up.

Closet Rehab Rule #5: Trust in Pump Power

Ordinary skirts, dresses and denim look extraordinary when paired with a hot pair of heels. But consider your comfort level, too, when purchasing footwear. If you're staggering along in those heels, you're not going to look, or feel confident. So, if you know you'll fear stepping out in spikes, opt for a wider, more comfortable heel.

Denizen

73 Thompson Street (btw. Spring and Broome Sts.)

SoHo 212-966-7299

Sometimes your best bets are virtually unknown. A local haven, Denizen serves up delightful French-Italian cuisine and flavored cosmos that go down sweet and smooth. Luxe booths, low lighting and elegant woodwork set a sensual scene. The staff is always happy to have you. The only thing missing: straight men, but that's why you bring your own. *Cosmos cost $9 (all flavors). Bartender's Pick: Peach Cosmo made with Stoli Peach, fresh lime juice, cranberry juice and sweet and sour ($9). Kitchen open Mon.-Sun. 5pm-2am. Appetizers: $6-$9, entrees: $15-$21.*

Fez

380 Lafayette St. (at Great Jones St.) East Village 212-533-7000

The intimate table setup at Fez makes it impossible for single mingling. You're on your own to look pretty on Moroccan inspired seats, complete with pillows. Try a light appetizer or cocktail (like the Flying Carpet) and enjoy the live musical performances, ranging from Indie to Jazz, on the lower level. In this setting, complete with beautiful tile work and luxe fabrics, you'll know why Fez is still glam after eight years. *Cosmos cost $7.50. Bartender's Pick: The Fez made with Absolut Citron, Chambord and fresh lime juice ($7.50). Time Café menu available Sun.-Thurs. 6pm-12pm, Fri.-Sat. 6pm-1am. Fez opens at 6pm.*

Open

559 West 22nd Street (at 11th Ave.) 212-243-1851

"Open what?" you may well ask. Well, for for starters, open your mind to going farther west than you've ever gone before. Then, open your mouth to enjoy European light bites like panini, cheese platters and smoked salmon. Next, open your eyes to co-owner Sylvain — he's cute as a button. Then keep those eyes open, as Sylvain's uber-design in the spirit of 50's airport lounge/industria-may give you a few tips for your own apartment. Open your ears, as the rotating DJs will be playing some unique tunes you probably won't hear elsewhere. And lastly, open your purse, because you'll have to take a cab home — you're in the middle of nowhere, for crying out loud. *Cosmos cost $8. Bartender's Pick: Open Martini made with vodka, lime juice, fresh mint, grenadine and a lump of sugar ($8). Kitchen open 12pm-5pm for lunch, and 5pm-2am for lounge menu ($8-$12).*

Temple Bar

332 Lafayette (at Bleecker St.) East Village 212-925-4242

According to the bartender, one Sapphire Martini ($12.25) will have you feeling good, but two is more than enough, so it's doubtful you'll be served a third. I know from a thorough investigation, that this is an entirely accurate account. A low-key ambiance, sleek and tastefully decorated, with high ceilings and a lounge area in back, Temple Bar is more of a date-spot than a schmoozing scene (although it is not blatantly romantic—so a good choice when you want to avoid the appearance of trying too hard), but is also perfect for friendly gatherings, since the bartenders are outgoing, and don't mind joining in on your chatter. You may be tempted to order an extravagant appetizer like caviar or oysters on the half shell, but if your wallet is hurting, you can fill up on the free popcorn, sprinkled with fried beets and yams. *Cosmos cost $10.25. Bartender's Pick: Sgroppino made with champagne, Skyy Citrus and lemon sorbet ($11). Appetizers served all night ($11-$32).*

YANG FOR EVERY YIN

As a good friend once told me, "It's a woman's right to make the rules. But then, it's also her right to change them." Therefore, while one day we wouldn't want a man hitting on us even if it turned out to be Derek Jeter, the very next day we may be up for some serious attention-grabbing. It's our right. So when you've been working out/got a new outfit/changed your 'do/got a makeover/need to piss off a guy, it's all about the excellent male to female ratio. These spots are testosterone tested and approved. So put on a happy face and get ready to act like you care about the stock market. (For happy hour man-meeting, turn to page 18).

Ike

103 2nd Ave. (at 6th St.) East Village 212-388-0388

Step back in time to an era when people apparently liked their drinks strong, but small. Ike brings back 50's style with a modern twist to the East Village with mini bites like a grilled brie and Cheddar sandwich or deviled eggs and fishsticks (not very sexy, but tasty all the same) that you'll kick yourself for eating in the morning. Lounge on a classic marshmallow sofa and sip mint juleps, sidecars or sloe gin fizzes ($7). *Cosmos cost $7. Bartender's Pick: June Bug made with Galliano vodka, pineapple juice, melon liqueur ($7). Kitchen open Mon. 5pm-1am, Tue.-Sat. 5pm-2am, Sun. 5pm-12am, weekend brunch served 12pm-5pm. Small plates: $6-$11, large plates: $9-$15.*

Light

129 E. 54th St. (btw. Park and Lexington Aves.)
Midtown 212-583-1333

Even the management will admit that there is a bit of a pick-up scene going on here. Since its opening in September of 2000, owners Andrew Sasson (of Jet Lounge, Jet East) and Chris Barish (Moomba) have been feeding patrons Asian-inspired appetizers like egg rolls and satay ($8-$12), and tasty house drinks like Apple Martinis ($11). DJs spin a wide range of lounge music Wednesday through Saturday. *Cosmos cost $9. Bartender's Pick: Apple Martini ($9). Appetizers served from 5pm-2am.*

Naked Lunch

17 Thompson St. (at Grand St.) West Village 212-343-0828

Inside past the velvet rope, a mingling scene teeming with phrases like "here's my card" and "did I mention I drive a Mercedes?" abounds. But, it's anyone's guess how those men got in, because the door policy does not work in their favor. Groups of men will not make it inside, even if accompanied by a female or two. And sneakers are unacceptable. The magic number behind the bar is 25 — that's the number of bottled beers and tequilas on the menu. On the weekends the vibe is classic 70's and 80's funk, R&B, Motown and new tunes. *Cosmos cost $8. Bartender's Pick: Top Shelf Margarita, made with a secret recipe ($9). Happy Hour Tues.-Fri. 5pm-9pm means $2 off drinks.*

Spread/At the Marcel Hotel

323 3rd Ave. (at 24th St.) Murray Hill 212-683-8880

Aside from the vulgarities that spring to mind when this bar's moniker is uttered, Spread should, by all conventions, be a trendy-hyped-Daily Candy-New York Magazine kind of place. It's located on the ground floor of a hotel. They serve sushi. If it looks like a duck and quacks like a duck, it's a duck right? Wrong. Never mind the ogling eyes (sometimes we like that, no?) and the roaming hands (hello people, you are in public), Spread misses the chichi mark — which is — partying into the wee hours. The place closes early, and clears out even before that. So, come early, while the boys hold court and the pickin's are ripe. *Cosmos cost $10. Bartender's Pick: Jude made with passion fruit purée, Chambord, orange juice with champagne ($12). Kitchen open from Mon.-Sat. 5pm-2am. Appetizers: $9-$16, entrees: $14-$22.*

Also check out these other swank-style bars, listed in the index, that rank high on the man meter: Cherry, Underbar, Spread, Wetbar, Whiskey Blue.

DARK DESTINATIONS

You have a pimple. You want to wear a blouse that the dry-cleaner could not remove the spot from. You haven't worked out in...a month (or two, or three, depending on who asks). You've burnt your upper lip attempting that at-home waxing that looked so simple in the infomercial. Bottom line—you don't want to be seen—all that clearly anyway. This is when the dark is our friend. These hotspots offer low lighting to accommodate any dermatological, hormonal, fitness-related, or sartorial complications.

Double Happiness

173 Mott St. (at Broome St.) Little Italy 212-941-1282

Double Happiness is located on a dark block, of the sort where it's best to have a taxicab drop you off right in front. Cavernous and well, small, you'll probably feel right at home here, except for the fact that there are hundreds of people packed in like they're at the Barneys Warehouse Sale. Appetizers (and now a few entrees) are available. Daily happy hour features 2 for 1 drinks from 6pm-7:30pm. *Cosmos cost $8. Bartender's Pick: Green Tea Martini made with citrus vodka, Cointreau, fresh lemon juice and green tea ($9). Appetizers: $6-$11, entrees: $12-$17.*

Idlewild

145 E. Houston St. (btw. 1st and 2nd Aves.)
Lower East Side 212-475-5005

There's no need to fasten your seatbelts in this airplane-themed boite, as it's nearly always empty with no eye candy to speak of. Drinks are listed on emergency instruction-like cards and even the WCs are fashioned after plane standards. If you're looking for laid-back, or just a place where you know you'll find a seat, Idlewild is the place to go. And its vicinity to scores of other LES hotspots means you can always head to a more hopping scene if you like. *Cosmos cost $9. Bartender's Pick: Idlewild made with citrus twist vodka, Cointreau, lime juice, Chambord and a splash of cranberry ($9).*

No. 9

109 E. 9th St. (btw. 3rd and 4th Aves.) East Village 212-529-5333

Under its former name, Pageant, this bar was NYU central. No. 9 has been elevated to a choice destination for twentysomethings with the help of new partner James Dezazzo of Asia de Cuba, 277 TriBeCa and the bar at Le Cirque. A full dinner menu is served until 12am. The serene second-floor lounge offers lots of seating options, like nooks of antique red-leather chairs surrounding small marble tables, and a mile-long sofa, chock full of eclectic throw pillows. No. 9 could easily go by chichi status, but the door policy is fair and the attitude just doesn't exist. Lounge open Tue.-Sun. with appetizers available until closing (choose delights like East Coast oysters, escargot and tuna tartare). *Cosmos cost $10 (Dezazzo insists he invented the drink). Bartender's Pick: Hendrick's Martini ($10). Kitchen open Thurs.-Sat. 5pm-12am, Sun.-Wed. 5pm-11pm. Appetizers: $8-$12, entrees: $5-$24.*

A Hole in One

I was never one to think that a gal could meet a boy of any merit at a bar. Smooching and smooching, and well, more smooching after cocktails and more cocktails had never been a successful recipe for me. Until one night. It was one of those nights when my hair looked like hell, my bloating had mysteriously added at least ten pounds to my normal body weight and absolutely nothing in my closet looked presentable. I didn't want to go out. I had worked all day and couldn't dream of sitting at a bar, attempting to talk to anyone about anything, other than how fat, depressed, overworked and under-clothed I was. But, you see, I'd made plans. I had a girlfriend who needed to go out. She was depressed about "Horse Teeth Boy" who had dumped her. I had a duty to perform.

I needed coffee. I needed an aspirin. I needed a goddamned new outfit. So, when she arrived at my house and I was wearing nothing but a bra and panties (very cute set, but somehow I couldn't imagine it was appropriate for the bar we were going to), she told me to "get my act together. Put on some stinking clothes and go." Ouch. She was right though, my current crisis didn't amount to a hill of beans in comparison to hers. I needed to gain some perspective. Quick. I made the mistake of throwing on something I hadn't worn in years. I thought it might do me good to change my look for the evening. But, what I hadn't realized was the gaping hole right on the derriere of the jeans. Apparently, neither had my friend.

When we arrived at Cherry, at one of the infamous W's,

many pairs of eyes were looking my way. When we finally made our way over to the bar, more eyes were looking my way. Gosh, maybe I look better than I'd realized, I thought. There was no seat available, so I stood behind a couple of guys at the back bar. Every time I'd scan the room, I noticed more men looking at me. There was pointing. There was smiling. My girlfriend, Cara, noticed it too and chalked it up to two hot chicks garnering appropriate amounts of attention.

We were halfway through working out the problem (coming to the conclusion that Horse Teeth Boy would have been a horrible choice of husband, since it was inevitable that his children would have a very good chance of inheriting the Horse Teeth gene, since that must, we concluded by a very scientific thought process, be a dominant trait), when I felt a tap on my shoulder.

"Um, you may want to think about covering your butt," said the stranger.

"What?" I asked, not quite sure I'd ever heard that pick up line before.

"Turn around honey," said Cara.

"Oh. My. God," she exclaimed. "Your entire ass is hanging out! When the hell was the last time you wore those jeans?"

I felt around the area in question. There, below the denim was flesh. Lots of it. About five inches of it. How could I have forgotten? That was why I stopped wearing those jeans in the first place!

"Err, thanks," I offered, brows arched. And then I booked. Full force to the loo. I was panicked. I looked at the accoutrements available at my disposal. I considered a quick MacGyver-ing tactic involving toilet paper. Too flimsy. Paper towel? How would I secure it? I opened my purse. Contents included: One pack of white Tic-Tacs, one pack of Parliaments, one wallet fitted with thirty dollars and forty-five cents, and one Christina Aguilera keychain securing five keys. I held onto the cigarettes shortly, but could not come up with any realistic remedy involving unrolled cigarettes, cardboard, or the damned clear plastic wrapping. Why, oh why had the Pashmina fad died out? It helped Gwyneth Paltrow in this exact instance! While I was fingering a twenty-dollar bill with a thoughtful look upon my face, Cara walked in.

"What the hell are you planning on doing with that?" she asked.

I had no answer to such a question.

"Take this and put it on," she instructed, Kingergarten-teacher style, as she handed me over a gorgeous charcoal-hued man's blazer. I couldn't help it. I looked at the label. Thomas Pink. I was impressed. I sniffed it. It smelled of yummy cologne. That was the closest I'd come to holding a man in quite some time. It was a bit overwhelming.

"Is it good enough for you? Girl, put the damn blazer on. That adorable guy who informed you about your, um, problem, asked that I bring it in here for you. He was going to come in himself, but the bouncer wouldn't let him."

"What? He really did that? Get out," I was shocked, checking my teeth for lipstick and slipping the jacket over my shoulders all at the same time. "Alright, let's go then," I said and started for the door.

"Hello McFly, just a minute."

"What now?" I asked, getting flustered.

"You might want to remove that toilet paper from your shoe," she suggested.

"Oh. Right."

What happened next was rather amazing. This adorable, sweet, intelligent boy named Alec (could you just die from a name like that?) bought me a drink. My wonderful, fabulous friend endured two hours talking to his not-quite-straight friend while I spoke with Alec about life, relationships, parents, the status of having HBO, how Nirvana was the most pivotal band since the Beatles, whether Courtney was in any way implicated in Kurt's untimely death, and exactly why my left butt cheek had been sticking out for the whole world to see.

At precisely 1:05 AM, he got very quiet, closed his eyes, leaned close to me, and...mmmm, kissed me very softly and sweetly. When the clock struck 2 and my friend had had just about enough of the not-quite-straight friend, she gave me the look a friend gives when she has clearly paid her dues. I had to wrap it up. But, wonder above all (even sample sales), he caught on, asked for my number—and promised to use it the next day. To take me out to dinner. "That is, if you could manage to dress properly." And I did. And he did. And yes, it was perfect. And yes, since he'd already seen my butt, I didn't find it that unreasonable for him to see it again. And again. And again. And if you'd like to know the rest of that story, Alec prefers that I leave our (yes our!) personal life, well, personal.

Reclaim your youth

There's a darned good reason why Toys R Us hasn't changed its slogan in decades. Nobody wants to grow up. Sure, at a certain age the romanticized vision of yourself, sprawled across your own couch, listening to Billie Holiday after feasting on a gourmet meal of your own making, free of the tyrannies of professors and resident advisors, seems like an arrangement that couldn't arrive soon enough. But once you've tossed your cap in the air and had your first taste of back-to-school shopping without going back to school, it becomes all too apparent that what you had been wishing away may in fact have been the best time of your life—and you know what that means—once again your mother was right.

While the prospect of going back for a second bachelor's, this time with the knowledge of exactly how to keep the Freshman Fifteen at bay, may seem an attractive one, chances are, this option is an impossibility. Instead of swapping your corporate card for a meal card and a bunk bed, spend a night at a college bar, or a bar where people act like they are still in college. You'll get to act as giddy as a school girl without having to write a thesis, mix with the co-eds without garnering a reputation, and when you wake up the next day with a hangover, you won't have to run into your suite-mate having sex in the adjoining room. So, make use of your own private bathroom, slip on a pair of hip-huggers, and remember the best part—you don't need to borrow anyone's ID.

These bars serve cheap drinks, and in the spirit, many offer shots as their bartender's pick for best drink. The majority of spots house pool tables, darts and other American pastimes. All, though, get loud and rowdy, call for casual attire, play the same songs that were popular when you were in college, and provide a plethora of opportunities for you to shed that corporate image and act like a kid again—so hop up on that bar top, drink that no-name vodka from a plastic cup and like it, and of course, don't forget to leave with a Zeta Psi.

Apple Bombar

17 Waverly Pl. (btw. Mercer and Greene Sts.)
West Village 212-473-8888

Apple Bombar's proximity to NYU ensures that lots of students are drinking away their tuition money here. While most are not sipping cognacs and downing the raw oysters on the menu, many are most likely widening their hops and barley knowledge with one of the Bôms (beer samplers), which offer five types of beer for $6. The testosterone-approved black, puffy leather couches are great for a happy hour gathering when Apple slashes one dollar (gee, thanks) off all beverages. *Cosmos cost $8. Bartender's Pick: Apple Martini ($8). Kitchen open Fri.-Sat. 12pm-12am, Mon.-Thurs. 12pm-11pm, Sun. 12pm-10pm. Appetizers: $4.95-$6.50, entrees: $8.95-$15.50.*

Bar East

1733 1st Ave. (btw. 89th and 90th Sts.)
Upper East Side 212-876-0203

Entertainment by way of pool, darts, sports on TV, and fresh popcorn. Choose from 8 tap and 8 bottled beers. *Cosmos cost $6. Bartender's Pick: Frozen Margarita ($6). Happy hour Mon.-Sun. 5pm-8pm with drinks specials like $2 Bud and Bud Light pints, $2 mixed drinks and $3 imported drafts.*

Big Easy (in the space of The Quiet Man)

1768 2nd Ave. (at 92nd St.) Upper East Side 212-348-0879

If you really want to escape the stresses of 9-to-5 living, call and inquire about guest bartending at The Big Easy on Thursdays. If you'd rather remain on the other side of the bar, though, you can enjoy cheap drinks, guess which patrons are underage, dance like it's spring break 4-eva and be as cheesy as you can be. In the summer months, save big bucks on $2.50 beers from 5pm-8pm daily, and on $1 Buds and well drinks from 9pm-10pm. Coming soon: A full menu with a bit of New Orleans flair. *Cosmos cost $6. Bartender's Pick: Hurricane made with Southern Comfort, rum, hurricane mix and crushed ice ($6).*

Bleecker Street Bar

58 Bleecker St. (at Crosby St.) West Village 212-334-0244

Old and musty and...perfect. Good music, good beers and good people. Play pool and waste your laundry quarters on the jukebox. *Cosmos cost $7. Bartender's Pick: Brooklyn Lager ($5 a pint). Happy hour Mon.-Sun. 12pm-8pm means $3.50 Miller Drafts (24 oz.).*

Bull's Head Tavern

295 3rd Ave. (btw. 22nd and 23rd Sts.) Gramercy 212-685-2589

Apparently residents of Murray Hill and Gramercy Park don't need a lot of sleep to get to work in the morning. Because any night of the week, Bull's Head has a wait for the two pool tables and it's three deep at the bar. Live bands play on certain nights and on the others a jukebox plays a wide variety of music from top 40 to classic rock. *Cosmos cost $8. Bartender's Pick: Margarita on the rocks ($6). Happy hour Mon.-Sun. 1pm-7pm means $3 frozen margaritas and draft pints (19 to choose from).*

Calico Jack's Cantina

800 2nd Ave. (btw. 42nd and 43rd Sts.) Midtown 212-557-4300

So, you want to feel like you're at the Jersey Shore, but you don't want to sit on the train for two hours? Voila, Calico Jack's Cantina to the rescue. Some may say cheesy, I say summer fun. The music's loud, there are five men to every woman and at least eight bright colors dominating the room. Love it or leave it, but don't leave without having at least one frozen margarita — especially on Thursday when they're half price until midnight — at which point they're free until close (and if you can slip out of work early on Fridays, you can catch one free drink hour from 5pm-6pm). *Cosmos cost $8. Bartender's Pick: Frozen blue Margarita with blue curacao ($8). Kitchen open Mon.-Fri. 11am-11pm, Sat.-Sun. 12pm-11pm. Appetizers: $4.95-$9.50, entrees: $6.95-$14.95.*

Dempsey's Pub

61 2nd Ave. (btw. 3rd and 4th Sts.) East Village 212-388-0662

You've only got five bucks and you want to go out? Head to Dempsey's before happy hour ends (7pm) and you can afford enough to catch a good buzz. NYU heaven, Dempsey's hosts fraternity parties from time to time. As Irish as a pub can get, the Old World charm makes the shabby, well, chic-ish à la book-lined walls and well-worn wood table tops. A back pool table, without the long wait, offers a good way to score some free beers. *Cosmos cost $6. Bartender's Pick: A pint of Guinness ($4.50).*

Dew Drop Inn

57 Greenwich Ave. (at Perry St.) West Village 212-924-2227

Southern hick style, the Dew Drop concocts potent, fruity cocktails galore ($7-9) in mason jars. Loud music and crowd seem to fade out after slinging a few. Kitchen serves up greasy eats in the Mexican-Cajun-American persuasions. In spring and summer grab an outside table on the front patio. *Cosmos cost $7 ($8 for top shelf). Bartender's Pick: Hawaiian Punch made with vodka, gin, rum, tequila, triple sec, amaretto, southern comfort, sloe gin, cranberry and pineapple juices ($9). Kitchen open from 12pm-1am on the weekends, 11pm weeknights. Happy hour Mon.-Fri. 4pm-7pm means $2 off all drinks. Appetizers: $4.50-$7, entrees: $5.50-$13.*

Dive 75

101 W. 75th St. (btw. Columbus and Amsterdam Aves.)
Upper West Side 212-362-7518

Games! Jenga, Connect 4 and checkers, which although lay unused in your closet at home, are surprisingly fun when accompanied by a beer (aren't so many things that way?) in a different environment — especially one with a jukebox to boot. If you're not in a beer mood, try a pint-sized margarita on the rocks for $9. Dive 75 also offers an assortment of cigars priced from $1-$12. If you're already uptown, make it a total dive bar night and stop by their other locations, The Dive Bar (732 Amsterdam Ave. at 96th St.; 212-749-4358), and The Broadway Dive (2662 Broadway at 101st St.; 212-865-2662). *Cosmos cost $8. Bartender's Pick: Vodka and cranberry juice ($5-$6). Ask for their menu book and order from any place that delivers. Happy hour Mon.-Sun. 5pm-7pm means $2.50 Buds, Bud Lights and $3.50 well drinks.*

Dorrian's Red Hand

1616 2nd Ave. (at 84th St.) Upper East Side 212-772-6660

If Dorrian's wasn't connected for all eternity with the 1986 Preppy Murder case, it would be just like any other over-aged frat bar. The red checkered tablecloths, cheap drinks, multiple televisions and typical bar fare — it's all standard operating procedures. If you're looking for this type of atmosphere, complete with a mostly male clientele (baseball caps, khakis and plaid shirts are plentiful), you won't be disappointed. *Cosmos cost $10. Bartender's Pick: Sex on the Beach made with vodka, peach schnapps, cranberry, grapefruit and pineapple juices ($6). Kitchen open Mon.-Sun. 11am-about 12am. Appetizers: $4.95-$9.95, entrees: $12.95-$14.95.*

Boy Begone

Get-away-quick strategies to save you from wasting time talking to men you don't want.

You know the deal. You're talking to your friend. You've given no signals of interest. That doesn't stop him. He wants to know your name. Do you come here often? What do you do? You're very good at pool. Do you live around here? You try to look away. You brush some imaginary lint from your pants. You mutter one-word answers. You talk to your friend whenever he gives you a second. He can't get a clue. Here, some field-tested techniques to get him to give it up.

- Concoct a fabricated version of your life involving Martians or inner voices.

- Indicate to him that the 300-pound bouncer is your boyfriend.

- Complain about how badly you want a boyfriend, someone who can really commit.

- Plead bathroom urgency and then relocate.

- Explain that you're involved in a clinical test that forbids you to shower for the next month.

- Talk about the new spring fashions.

- Introduce the subject of your ex-boyfriend.

- Divulge your two-year plan of getting married and having three children.

- Describe the details of the strange "rash" you have contracted.

- Tell him that you are saving yourself for your husband.

- Assure him that you'd love to stay and chat but your baby sitter gets off in an hour.

Down The Hatch

179 W 4th St. (btw. 6th and 7th Aves.) West Village 212-627-9747

If you don't want to work on your thesis, or you just want to act like you still have a thesis to write, head over for wings, burgers and beer and watch the game. You can also play your own game of darts, foosball and various video games, or get ogled by the predominantly male/drunk patrons. On Saturdays and Sundays, you can play guess who will fall off their barstool first, when $16 buys you three pitchers of beer and all of the wings you can eat (1pm-6pm). There's nothing quite like ordering a burger at the side window, and carrying it back to your seat for everyone to see (waitress service Thurs.-Sat. only). *Cosmos cost $7. Bartender's Pick: Route 9 made with Malibu, Chambord, Stoli Peach, cranberry and pineapple juices and 7Up, served in a mug ($6). Kitchen open Mon.-Sun. 12pm-an hour before closing. Food: $6-$25.*

Finnerty's (formerly Looking Glass)

108 3rd Ave. (btw. 13th and 14th Sts.) East Village 212-777-3363

When this bar was called Looking Glass, my friend nicknamed it, "Looking for Ass," which is still quite on the mark. Predominantly a student hangout, Finnerty's is a basement-level bar with a small garden out back. Doors open at 11:30am, so it's a great spot to hit when you're really shirking responsibilities and decide to ditch work. *Cosmos costs $6. Bartender's Pick: Long Beach Iced Tea made with vodka, gin, rum, tequila, triple sec, sour mix and cranberry juice ($6 for a pint glass). Mon.-Sun. from open to close $2 pints of Bud, Bud Lite and McSorley's. Sun. $3 Bloody Marys.*

The Gin Mill

442 Amsterdam Ave. (btw. 81st and 82nd Sts.)
Upper West Side 212-580-9080

Any bar where the bartender says, "We need more women because I get tired of entertaining all of the men in here," is absolutely a fantastic bar in my opinion. And to entice us ladies, Tuesday night is our night, with dollar margaritas and beers for females. Plenty of bar food to munch on (from hot pretzels to a tuna steak), and 28 beers to choose from. Entertainment (other than the male sort) includes foosball, golf game, and pool, in addition to 13 televisions playing every sporting event imaginable. Columbia students, quarter-life and mid-life crisis sufferers all drink in harmony, while listening to classic rock (except on Thursdays when bands and comedy acts take the stage). *Cosmos cost $7. Bartender's Pick: Mind Eraser made with Kalhua, Absolut and Club Soda — layered ($5.50). Kitchen open Mon.-Sun. 11:30am-2am. Food: $1.50-$9.50.*

Googie's

237 Sullivan St. (at W. 3rd St.) West Village 212-673-0050

If your name is not already carved into one of Googie's tabletops, well by God, it should be. Greasy eats are served up hot and fast, and the drinks keep flowing. College students have been wasting precious study time here for over three decades, and it's pretty obvious why. Games are always on the tube, the bartenders and waitresses are friendly, and most people don't leave until they've eaten more free peanuts than they care to recall (if they could). And happy hour drink specials from 5-8pm like $2 pints of Bud, Bud Light and Killian's don't hurt either. *Cosmos cost $5.50. Bartender's Pick: Kamikaze shot ($5.50). Kitchen open Fri.-Sat. 11:30am-12am. Appetizers: $4.50-$7.50, entrees: $7.50-$16.*

Madame X

94 W. Houston St. (btw. LaGuardia and Thompson Sts.)
West Village 212-539-0808

In this competitive bar scene, sometimes it helps to have an angle. And the concept of a French bordello smack in the middle of the Village is just as good as any. To support the theme, the specialty drink menu offers lots of not-so-subtle cocktails like Pussy Galore, Orange You Glad You Came, and Cherry Pop ($7-$9). Climb the stairs to the newly renovated second level lounge, complete with loads of leopard-print, reds, dim lamps and a new atrium, which overlooks the back garden (open seasonally). Here NYU students and those attempting to act like students try not to grind to the top-notch dance music — since this bar sadly lacks a cabaret license. *Cosmos cost $8. Bartender's Pick: Rum Strip and Go Naked made with Kaniche rum, Myer's rum, Malibu rum and Cruzan pineapple rum ($9). Cover $5 Fri.-Sat. after 10pm.*

MacDougal Ale House

122 MacDougal St. (btw. Bleecker and W. 3rd Sts.)
West Village 212-254-8569

Since its opening in 1997, NYU students have taken control, and never given up the reins. The typical co-ed allure by way of pool, darts and Eric Clapton on the jukebox proves a winning combination. For a more private gathering, grab a table in back. When you want to escape the city, walk downstairs to MacDoug's, where the lighting is low, the staff is friendly, and the environment is so laid-back, you may never want to leave. *Cosmos cost $6. Bartender's Pick: Jack and Coke ($5). Sun.-Wed. $2 pints of Budweiser and $7 all day from 12pm on.*

Nevada Smith's

74 3rd Ave. (btw. 11th and 12th Sts.) East Village 212-982-2591

When I was in college, this was one of the few bars that would serve us. Apparently, the same still holds true. The Irish bartenders are sweet and fast and most all sporting events are televised. Some things have changed over the years though; a downstairs lounge has been added and the bathrooms have received a much-needed makeover. *Cosmos cost $7. Bartender's Pick: A pint of Magners ($5). Happy Hour Mon.-Fri. 11:30am-7pm means $3 pints of Bud and Bud Lite. Sun., Tue., Thurs. $2 Michelob 7pm to closing, and all of the karaoke (see also page 115) you can take.*

No Idea

30 E. 20th St. (btw. Broadway and Park Ave. S.)
Gramercy 212-777-0100

Don't even think about coming to this bar when you want to feel like a grown up (Gramercy Tavern is a couple of doors down for that). Definitely consider No Idea when you're in the mood to practice some flirting, expand your business card collection, do shots, play pool and dance to run-of-the mill party songs. Also consider hitting the bar on summer Saturday nights when wearing your old bridesmaid dresses gets you free drinks from 7pm-12am — you can't feel any less adult than when you're doing that — that is, doing anything and everything for free drinks. Also scan their name-night calendar (posted on the window outside) for your own name; stop in when yours is on the list and score complimentary cocktails from 5pm-11pm (first, last and middle are all fair game). *Cosmos cost $7.50. Bartender's Pick: Stoli Raspberry and 7Up ($6.50 for pint-sized glass). Ask for their menu book and order take-out from any place that delivers.*

Off The Wagon

109 MacDougal St. (btw. W. 3rd and Bleecker Sts.)
West Village 212-533-4487

Order up a Screaming Ted shot as soon as you arrive. You'll need it to tolerate the noise of overworked NYU grad students who may or may not have passed the bar/their final thesis/their loan application. A typical grad and undergrad hangout, Off The Wagon has satellite TV and cable to air all of the games, and two pool tables upstairs where a second bar comes in handy to keep your tongue wet between shots. There is a full menu with all the staples, like wings and burgers, to help you harken back to the time when you didn't count the carbs and fat grams in each morsel of food you ate . Daily promotions keep cheap drinkers happy; stop in for happy hour Mon.-Fri. 4pm-8pm, when all beverages are half price, or on Ladies Night for $1 and $1.50 drafts (choose from 14 varieties) from 8pm-closing Wednesdays. *Cosmos cost $7. Bartender's Pick: Ted's Punch — a top secret recipe that contains 8 types of alcohol and a mixture of fruit juices that tastes like 5-Alive ($6). Kitchen open Mon.-Fri. 2pm-4am, Sat.-Sun. 12pm-4am. Food: $5.95-$12.*

Fun With Business Cards

gratifying things to do with the business cards of men you never heard from

God, how those useless bits of cardboard seem to pile up. The worst thing you can do is to keep them lying around. Everyone gets to a point when they start digging through old phone books and stacks of paper looking for someone (anyone, please) to phone, even if it's just for the purpose of checking that you are still alive. At those times, phone your friends, call your credit card company to find out about lowering your APR, even call your mother for heaven's sake…but don't call that bloke who passed you his card six months ago, before mispronouncing your name and swaggering out the door with his tie over his shoulder.

There are, however, plenty of things you can do with those paper scraps that are useful. With scads of time under my belt spent staring at those cards printed with useless phrases like, "Coordinator of this" or "Chaser of that" or "Vice President of Absolutely Nothing Important," I've come up with a few uses for you.

- Paint over each one using a different color. When dry, use a hot glue gun to run a patterned ribbon along one side of the cards (leaving about three inches between each). Hang the ribbons around the tops of your walls. Voila...you've got a cute border for your room.

- Recycle, recycle. But, before you do, add the emails to your address book so that you'll always have enough addresses to mail those horrifying chain letters to. If they don't forward it to ten people in 24 hours, perhaps they will never find love!

- Forward them to a dating service.

- Send them to a telemarketing agency.

- Bring them to the winter solstice ritual and throw them all into the bonfire.

- Make a decoupage candleholder for your relaxation candle.

- Glue them together (stacked one on top of another) and paint over them for a paperweight.

- Sign each of the names up for community service projects. Chances are, at least a few will buckle and do the good deed when they're called for duty.

Ryan's

151 2nd Ave. (btw. 9th and 10th Sts.) West Village 212-979-9511

An Irish pub located right near two NYU dorms, hmm…yes, Ryan's draws a crowd pretty much all of the time. Have a pint and practice your Gaelic with the staff while you marvel at exactly how many different incarnations Guinness paraphernalia is available in. Ryan's regulars appreciate the good food, reasonable drink prices, and in the warmer months—the outdoor seating. *Cosmos cost $7. Bartender's Pick: Metropolitan, a cosmo made with Absolut Currant ($7). Kitchen open Sun.-Wed. 12pm-11pm, Thurs.-Sat. 12pm-1am. Appetizers: $5.95-7.95, entrees $9.95-$14.95. Happy hour Mon.-Fri. 12pm-7pm for $2 domestic bottles, $3 beers and mixed drinks. Sat and Sun. at bar $3.50 pints and mixed drinks.*

Shades of Green

125 E. 15th St. (btw. Irving Pl. and 3rd Ave.)
Gramercy 212-674-1394

A not-much-to-mention pub design. A non-descript drink menu. Complimentary Chex Mix. A shining example of how sometimes less is more. A regular NYU spot, which gets lots of business due to the dorms nearby, you'll get to have your ID checked and all. Wear jeans. Don't do your hair. Have a beer. Invent an exotic major. *Cosmos cost $5.50. Bartender's Pick: Shades of Green Special—all they're saying is it's good and it's green ($5). Kitchen open Mon.-Sun. 11:30am-11pm for homemade Irish fare (appetizers about $5.95; entrees range from $6.95-$16.95). Closed Sun. in summer. Happy hour free buffet Mon.-Fri. 5pm-7pm.*

Third & Long

523 3rd Ave. (at 35th St.) Murray Hill 212-447-5711

80/20 male to female ratio. Lack of décor. Numerous television sets. Irish staff. Bathrooms in the basement. Yes, this is a sports bar. It's a great place to watch a game. That is, when you can't get in anywhere else. Recently, Third & Long has done a bit of painting and primping, along with the addition of more seats. Stop in on Wednesdays for live music. You can even have a beer for a buck on Mondays and Tuesdays. Saturday all drinks are half off for ladies. Happy hour specials run from 11am-8pm most nights. *Cosmos cost $7. Bartender's Pick: Carmel Apple Martini sweetened up with a bit of caramel ($7).*

Tin Lizzie's

1647 2nd Ave. (btw. 85th and 86th Sts.)
Upper East Side 212-288-7983

Upper East Siders don't seem to venture beyond a four-block radius, which is why awful bars like this one stay in business. But, hey, if you can't beat 'em, join 'em. And once you're there, you'll see the upside to tossing your heels aside for the night and replacing them with a pair of flip-flops. So what if the bar is a hole in the wall? If you can dance to Biggie Smalls and sing all of the words out loud, down a couple of shots and not feel the need to check your lipstick once—have you really missed anything? *Cosmos cost $5. Bartender's Pick: Kamikaze shot ($4).*

Bar Crawls

The very phrase conjures up images of plastic cups and groups of drunk persons meandering the streets in search of cheap beer—ahh, youth!

Lindy Promotions organizes bar crawls in various Manhattan districts twice each year (in Spring and Fall), in which anyone over 21 can take their cup to all of the bars on the tour and receive extremely reasonable drinks like $2 drafts and $3 mixed drinks on Saturday afternoons. Register for one in your area (Upper West Side, Upper East Side, Greenwich Village or Midtown East), or sign up for all of the crawls in all of the areas. For the past 10 years, serious youth-reclaimers have been enjoying these beer fests. Registration is completed at the first bar on the lineup, with a five-hour window to prevent long lines. Participants receive a 16-oz cup for the registration fee (about $11), and a $3 discount if two canned food items are donated. For details, log onto www.lindypromo.com.

Stealing Hottie

I guess sometimes you just want to indulge any whim you may have without consequence. This urge frequently occurs when you've had too much of being an adult. Now we don't have to blame ourselves. Now we can blame our quarter-life crisis. Thank God! It's just so much simpler than taking responsibility for childish actions. Racking my brain for immature, purely selfish acts was difficult (I, like yourself, I have no doubt, am normally angelic in nature, flawless in action and thought), but I decided to share this year's most base behavior with you all, since much of the action took place in bars, and since you can all learn from (or empathize with) this chain of events.

In the beginning: Girl meets boy with serious girlfriend. Girl runs into this boy quite often to pursue innocent chitchat with not-so-innocent undertones (smiles, references to men and indecent behavior, exaggeration of current state of success and celebrity) on the subway, at shops and outside various public establishments. Boy is apparently enticed. Girl begins foaming at the mouth at odd times. For six months both impersonate perfectly upstanding citizens save for the occasional shared daydream involving Jell-O, whipped cream and various toys, which can be purchased at stores on West 4th Street named after racy felines.

Sometime after that: Girl experiences the sort of month where circle of friends has mysteriously dwindled, magazines that provided rent-paying assignments have gone out of business and men have apparently developed fatal allergies to her that require maintaining a 10-mile

distance, resulting in extreme lack of dates. On the night when we join her, she has already watched *16 Candles, Pretty in Pink* and *She's Having a Baby*, and is quite prepared to dye her hair red and begin wearing too much pink if that is what it takes to garner attention from the opposite sex. Instead, she draws the shades, places an order for Pluck U under an assumed name and stocks up on Chubby Hubby. After feast and self-pity session she feels the sudden urge to clean everything in sight. Pulling together all of her clothing, girl drags body-bag sized load of laundry to the laundromat. In God-altered series of events, said boy appears out of nowhere and invites girl to visit friend's bar later in the evening. Quickly calculating scientific equation that measures necessity to act like moral upstanding citizen, and weighs figure against need to get out of apartment and spend time with male companion, said girl finds foreign voice using her mouth as its instrument to agree to midnight meeting.

At undisclosed bar listed in Reclaim Your Youth section (names left out to protect the not-innocent): In immediate-gratification sort of twist, girl becomes object of desire and—at risk of sounding desperate—love at 20th sight, expressed through emotion-induced hand squeezes, long, deep stares and arm possessively placed over shoulders. Girl is speechless. Okay, maybe not speechless, since conversation flows incessantly re: adolescent tragedy, family complications, and idyllic profiles of future life partners.

At next undisclosed bar listed in Reclaim Your Youth section: Girl downs fourth Red Bull and Vodka and second shot of tequila. Girl and boy engage in not-so-appropriate public displays of affection. Girl swoons at sight of muscular ex-football player (hers!) returning from the bar. Boy's green eyes (the greenest she's ever seen on a human being?) burn hole into girl's heart. Girl is more than ready to put aside former pledges against sleeping with someone else's boyfriend. Girl wonders if boy will be able to wear extra-large condoms in bedside drawer?

After sun has begun to rise: Boy and girl whisper in hallway as girl fumbles with keys while foreign hand begins to creep up thigh creating tingles and jingles (of keys).

A whole two and a half hours later!: Girl inhales cigarette deeply while holding in stomach, wondering what she will call their first-born and realizing for the first time that sex can last longer than five minutes!

A few weeks later: Time proves that men, despite claims to the contrary, will not leave girlfriends for mistresses. But, that booty-calls can be empowering and that upon further consideration, one would not want to spend life with dishonest cheater who shows no remorse for cheating on girlfriend.

The User-Friendly Boogie

If you want to dance, but can't stomach the hard-core, high-priced club scene, read on for bars with dance floors that play music you actually know the words to. You can get into all of these places without the hassles associated with clubs—these have no lists, no hour-long lines, nor hefty $25 covers. As with clubs, though, you'd do best to call ahead to check the musical line-up for the night if your tastes are very specific—as DJs and musical genres tend to change from time to time.

Asylum

149 Bleecker St. (btw. Thompson St. and LaGuardia Pl.)
West Village 212-254-8492

It's filthy, and packed in with students and B&Ts, but, even I can make the best of a place as long as it's got a good DJ. If you've got the need to bust a move, head over to this underground bar, where Hip-Hop-Hooray is always on the lineup (and don't forget the hand sanitizer). *Cosmos cost $8. Bartender's Pick: Malibu Bay Breeze made with Malibu and pineapple and cranberry juices ($6). Happy hour Wed.-Sat. 4pm-9pm all drinks $3. Cover Fri.-Sat $5 for women, $10 for men, Wed.-Thurs. $5 for everyone. Tuesday is 80's night, Wed.-Sat. a mix of hip-hop, R&B, classic dance and rock 'n roll.*

Drinkland

339 E. 10th St. (btw. Aves. A and B) East Village 212-228-2435

One of the pioneers of the Alphabet City Chic trend, Drinkland remains strong in its fifth year. Inside, the graphic black and white design and always-crowded space make it impossible to stay for more than a couple of rounds. Although the electronic music is hot, it is not likely you'll find lots of room to shake your thang. If you tire of the battle for floor space settle for a seat at one of the booths while rumps bump you in the head. Otherwise head to the side room for a bit of a quieter, lounge locale. Check out their Sunday night drum and bass party. *Cosmos cost $7. Bartender's Pick: Rum Punch made with light and dark rums, three fruit juices and lime juice ($6). Closed Mondays. Electronic music exclusively. Cover on Sundays only: $5.*

Eugene's

27 W. 24th St. (btw. 5th and 6th Aves.) Chelsea 212-462-0999

The 40's supper club motif translated into oversized booths, mahogany-a-plenty, and lots of indoor foliage caused a bit of a stir when first Eugene's opened its doors. Now, it is almost impossible to appreciate any of those amenities, what with the 20-minute wait for drinks, disorganization that plagues the door patrol and continuously rude bartenders. In the past months, they've added a cover charge certain nights, that makes it much more difficult to make excuses for this spot. The only one I can think of: you can dance. *Cosmos cost $11. Bartender's Pick: Sour Apple Martini ($11). Cover Thurs.-Sat. $20 after 10pm. For dinner, reservations are suggested. Kitchen open for dinner Thurs.-Sat. 6pm-12am. Lounge menu available from 5pm-2am. Closed Sun.-Mon. New menu coming soon.*

Eau

913 Broadway, 2nd Floor (btw. 20th and 21st Sts.)
Flatiron 212-358-8647

Eau is one of the best spots to boogy down late night. Upstairs from Punch, Eau's DJs spin new and old-school hip-hop, which keeps patrons bumping and grinding way into the wee hours. Head over when you are sick of dancing with boys who don't know how to move it. No cover and reasonably priced drinks are unexpected bonuses, as are the accommodating bouncers and bartenders. No matter how much of a wallflower you may be, you won't be able to resist the urge to cut the rug. *Cosmos cost $8. Bartender's Pick: Martini ($9). Cover on Sat. $10 after 10pm.*

Gonzales Y Gonzales

625 Broadway (btw. Bleecker and Houston Sts.)
West Village 212-473-8787

The sin city-inspired neon sombrero, with its colorful flashing lights, ensures that no passersby could possibly fail to notice this Mexi-chic restaurant/club. A full dinner menu is easily out classed by other NYC south-of-the-border eateries (and doesn't come cheap). But Gonzales Y Gonzales devotees are not in it for the quesadillas. Frosty bevs (9 flavors of frozen margaritas at $7.50 each) go down smooth, and live Latin, Salsa and Meringue music, (starting at 9:30pm Wed.-Thurs.; 11:30pm Fri.-Sat.), brings droves of party-seekers to shake their rumps well after they've lost the ability to judge how well they move. *Cosmos cost $8. Bartender's Pick: Black cherry and mango frozen margarita ($7.50). Kitchen open 12pm-2am Fri.-Sat., Sun.-Thurs. 12pm-12am. Appetizers: $4-$7, entrees: $10-$15.*

Groovejet NYC/(formerly Jet Lounge)

286 Spring St. (btw. Hudson and Varick Sts.) SoHo 212-929-4780

Owner Greg Brier, the South Beach legend behind Rose Bar, Rebar, and Velvet, opens the doors of his brand new dance lounge, Groovejet NYC, in the fall of 2001. You can expect, I was told, "futuristic fabrics," lots of dark woods, plush couches, a fireplace, and designs of local "street-wise" artists. The company also says that the digital surround sound music system they've implemented is the first of its kind. Other high-tech extras include eight flat-screen monitors playing trippy graphics that bounce along to the beat, and beat-driven light shadows illuminating the dance floor. Doubtless, all of this equipment was designed with the top-name DJs Brier often works with in his other musical ventures, in mind — the ubiquitous Fat Boy Slim was one name dropped. Expect lots of electronica Thursday through Saturday. Brier promises no cover and no velvet rope will darken the scene. *Cosmos cost $7. Bartender's Pick: Groovejet Martini made with chilled Ketel One and lychee nuts ($9). Kitchen open from 5pm-dawn. Appetizers range from $4-$8, entrees: $10-$16.*

Guernica

Avenue B (btw. 2nd and 3rd Sts.) East Village 212-674-0984

Due to the current trendiness of this strip, Guernica gets packed on the weekends with those who consider the East Village the nightlife mecca. Upstairs the restaurant serves American cuisine with a "Pan-Asian" flair until midnight, when the space becomes a quieter refuge from the disco downstairs. For a five-dollar cover on weekends, you can dance to the current favorites between concrete columns (watch out once you've begun drinking). Weekdays range from techno (Monday) to Drum and Bass (Tuesday) to Two-Step and UK Garage (Wednesday) to Electronica (Thursday). Sunday through Thursday start the night out early, and save on two for one drinks from 6pm-9pm. *Cosmos cost $8.50. Bartender's Pick: Apple martini ($8.50). Kitchen open Mon.-Sun. 6pm-12am. Appetizers: $6-$12, entrees: $11-$18. Fri. and Sat. $5 cover after 10pm.*

Lansky Lounge and Grill

104 Norfolk St. (btw. Delancey and Rivington Sts.)
Lower East Side 212-677-9489

In this very downtown speakeasy, complete with clandestine-style entrance through a back alley to an unmarked door, you'll find lots of Upper East Siders and commuter folk who come to get down to the dance-worthy music. Located at the rear of Ratner's, Lansky recently took over more space, which means more room to sip martini drinks and get down. Even though the spot is filled with down-to-earth sorts, Lansky hosts its fair share of celeb soirées. Music varies nightly from hip-hop to classic 70's to live Jazz, with Paul Sevigny spinning on Thursdays ($5 cover). *Cosmos cost $9. Bartender's Pick: Mikado made with Stoli raspberry, fresh raspberry puree, triple sec and lime juice ($9). Happy Hour Mon.-Fri. 6pm-8pm offers half price martinis.*

Madison's Nite Club

1584 York Ave. (btw. 83rd and 84th Sts.)
Upper East Side 212-570-5454

Alright, so the guys wear more jewelry than the girls, and the majority are named Joey or Frankie, but they're cute, okay? Plus, you can dance to traditional dance hits by Biggie and friends and act like you're on spring break. For a $10 cover on Fridays and $12 on Saturdays, those 21 and over get to act like teenagers and collect many telephone numbers for emergency dateless situations. *Cosmos cost $7. Bartender's Pick: Seabreeze made with vodka, cranberry and orange juices ($6). Happy hour Fri. 7pm-10pm means reduced priced drinks.*

McFadden's

800 2nd Ave. (at 42nd St.) Midtown 212-986-1515

Save your Manolos sister, because this huge Jersey/Long Island style bar packs a crowd that won't know a Gucci from a Pucci. Even so, over-aged frat boys can be fun. So dance it up or grab a seat in back (if you can get past the VIP bouncer) and act like you're 18 again. Fridays and Saturdays, DJs play classic dance music. Other nights come in to watch sporting events on the ten satellite televisions. If you can't pick up at least one drunk stockbroker, you should really ask for a refund. *Cosmos cost $7. Bartender's Pick: Belvedere martini made with vodka and dry vermouth ($7). Kitchen open Mon.-Sun. 11:30am-11am. Appetizers range from $5-$11, entrees: $10-$14. Cover is $5 on Saturdays.*

Potion Lounge

370 Columbus Avenue (at 78th St.) Upper West Side 212-721-4386

With a Space-Age design, an intimate atmosphere, no cover, and small, yet spacious dance floor, Potion is a great spot for getting a groove on. DJ spins a mix of dance music (hip-hop, R&B, and classics) on Fridays and Saturdays. Big comfy tables are perfect for resting your tired feet and munching on chicken quesadillas, fried calamari or pizzas, while sipping their gravity-defying layered cocktails. Usually this space is not too crowded late-night, which means you can dance without embarrassment, and grab a seat without too much waiting. *Cosmos cost $10. Bartender's Pick: Love Potion made with cranberry, lime and orange juices, peach schnapps and vodka ($10). Appetizers range from $6-$12. Kitchen open Tue.-Thurs. 6pm-12am, Fri.-Sat. 6pm-2am.*

Sapphire Lounge

249 Eldridge St. (btw. Houston and Stanton Sts.)
Lower East Side 212-777-5153

Before hipsters invaded the LES, Sapphire Lounge was making waves in the dancing world. This was never a classy joint. Nobody ever said it was. But if you like to dance, you will love it. There is not much of it to love — your freshman dorm room was larger (yes, it was) — but what there is, a down-to-earth sort who wants to get her freak on will truly admire. Chichi need not apply. Monday 7pm-10pm drinks are half price. Saturdays is classic house, reggae, R&B, Latin and funk. Admission price varies, but it's never more than $5. *Cosmos cost $7. Bartender's Pick: Sapphire Rose made with Sapphire gin, rosewater, and sweet lemon juice ($7).*

Slipper Room

167 Orchard St. (at Stanton St.) Lower East Side 212-253-7246

A relative newcomer to the Lower East Side, the Slipper Room is full of the energy and diversity that LES spots bring to the plate. Retro through and through, Fridays reintroduce the 80's via old favorites mixed with new tracks in a way that is anything but ordinary. The entertainment lineup here ranges from DJs to vaudeville to cabaret, bands and theater pieces, so make sure to call ahead. *Cosmos cost $7. Bartender's Pick: Dirty Martini $7-$10 depending on vodka. Appetizers: $4-$7. Kitchen open Tue.-Sat. 8pm-12am.*

Tavaru

195 3rd Ave. (at 17th St.) Gramercy 212-471-9807

Mad River's previous proprietor team decided to transplant an Upper East Side bar formula below 20th Street. Surprisingly enough, it worked. It's packs in on weekends, so you'll have to stake your territory in the small space to dance to the Destiny's Child-esque tunes. Tavaru has recently upgraded, adding a bit of bamboo here and a bunch of back tables there to accommodate diners indulging in tapas and thin-crust pizzas. While eye candy is a luxury here, there are at least six guys to every girl, and lets face it, that just ups your free drink potential. Or you can really up your free drink potential by playing guest bartender most nights of the week. *Cosmos cost $8. Bartender's Pick: Tavaru made with Mount Gray Rum, Myers Dark Rum, Peach Schnapps, grenadine, orange and pineapple juices ($8). Kitchen open 12pm-10pm daily. Appetizers: $8-$11, entrees: $8-$12. Happy hour Mon.-Fri. 12pm-6pm, with daily specials. Guest bartending Wed.-Sat. DJs Thurs.-Sat.*

A Spy from the Other Team

How many times have you pondered the male psyche in an attempt to decode men's cryptic behavior? Why didn't he call? What was he thinking? How would he react if I went up and talked to him? To enlighten us on these and other burning questions, I've enlisted *Men's Health* Deputy Editor Stephen Perrine.

Girl's Guide: Do men ask a woman for her number if they don't intend to use it, and if so, why?

Stephen Perrine: Sometimes. Usually, they sorta, kinda intend to use it, but we're often afraid that when you've sobered up, you'll also wise up. Also, a lot of guys are just plain lazy. But sometimes asking for a number is a conquest thing: she likes me, I got her number, I'm cool. Guys in relationships will do this as a harmless (to them, at least) way of proving they're still attractive to the opposite sex.

GG: When men say, "I'll call you soon," how many days does "soon" really mean?

SP: Mm…two or three days.

GG: So, does that mean there actually is a "two-day rule" for calling women? And, if so, what is the reasoning behind it?

SP: Yes, there is, because if we call you the next day, you're going to think we're a) desperate; b) a potential stalker; c) somehow otherwise undesirable. If you women would actually react positively to a next-day phone call, we'd call. But you don't, so we wait—after we've been burned the first few times, that is.

GG: If a girl is with a group of female friends, is that intimidating for guys?

SP: Depends. Usually a guy can throw himself into a large group with a reasonable chance of success with at least one of them. What's difficult is when you meet a girl who seems to be alone, and then she brings you over and introduces you to her group of friends. Then you're like a carcass in the desert. They'll just pick you apart.

GG: If a girl is with a group of males, would a man ever consider talking to her?

SP: Hell no.

GG: Does a man like it when a woman takes the initiative and approaches him first?

SP: Yes. Almost all guys think this is fine; it takes so much pressure off, you'll often find the guy you approach will be more honest and "real" than a guy who makes the first move.

GG: How much do men assume about a woman from the way she's dressed?

SP: It's more class than anything about her sexually. Skin tight designer dress? Class. Skintight acid-wash jeans? Drop the "cl."

GG: Do you think men seriously consider dating women they meet in a bar setting?

SP: I think that depends on what she's like, what you're like, and where you are at any given stage of your life. If you're just looking for a good time, anyone will do. If you're looking for something you can build on, then it's fine too, as long as she's relatively together and not a drunken mess by the end of the evening. I have children, so I won't get involved with anyone who appears the least bit daft. But sane people go to bars, too.

GG: Why do you think guys oftentimes use a prepared line?

SP: I'm not aware that we do. Then again, I had to sit and prepare that response.

Dancing Fool

My mother tells me that I was conceived while she and my father were following the Grateful Dead around the country, selling concert tee-shirts from the back of their van. As a young child, I would wear the leftover tees around the house, with my little toes and fingers barely visible beneath the skull-emblazoned garments. I cite this as the foundation for my profound, yet troubling, love of music. I say "troubling" because for all of my devotion, I could never sing, master a musical instrument or perform any other action that would render me a music aficionado. I always held strong, though.

Year after year, I tried all of the common things one does to express their loyalty to the culture. In my Heavy Metal stage, I wore tie-dyed Led Zeppelin tee-shirts and aptly distressed denim, and watched *The Song Remains The Same* 315 (and a half) times. I dated a metal-head, a.k.a. dirtbag. I tried to smoke pot (but never learned how to inhale properly). When the New Wave took over, I dressed the part with striped tights and Doc Martins and wore my WDRE pin with pride. Still later, I deciphered every word of the Fresh Prince's youth rebellion theme song, "Parents Just Don't Understand." I was one of the first people to stand in line to purchase Pearl Jam's *Ten*. Although I enjoyed those so-called "musical" experiences, I never quite felt I was actually part of the music. Along the way, I had tried a number of active approaches to musical integration.

In the third grade a music program was founded in my school, and with fantasies of Carnegie Hall in my head,

I insisted on the violin. Only, my father had saved his clarinet over the years, so my parents thought my following in his footsteps would be a wonderful way to carry on a family tradition. All of that blowing proved too tiresome for my cheeks, and "She'll be coming around the Mountain," the only song I'd mastered, was not much to my tastes anyway. Visions of Broadway came my way the following year, when my teacher announced we'd be putting on a production of Cinderella. But, no matter how much I Bibbidi-Bobbidi-Boo'd before the rehearsal, I'd only been able to score a part on the props committee (and that was after my mother had gone up to talk to Mrs. Stangler).

By the seventh grade (when I'd failed to make the orchestra, band or choir), I'd begun looking outside of school for my musical outlets. Finding a dusty old Yamaha in our attic, I signed myself up for guitar lessons. I recorded a tape of songs I wanted to learn how to play. I made regular visits to the Long Island Guitar Center to flirt with the long-haired object of my pubescent crush, and non-incidentally invested in a pair of barely legal cutoff jean shorts purchased at the sadly no-longer-existent Antique Boutique, here in the city. The spoils of my one-year endeavor? One thoroughly handled photograph of my long-haired crush, a dusty guitar that I never learned to string, much less play, and one cassette that serves as a time capsule of 1989 (does anyone remember Trixter?).

It was time to re-evaluate. Did I have the music in me? Anywhere? It was around that time that I began reading the biographies of rock legends to garner a clearer picture of the various places one could fit in on the scene. That is when I learned about groupies. Of course! I couldn't believe it hadn't struck me earlier. I could become a very famous groupie, perhaps even muse, to one of the great musicians of our time, and there- by an integral part of the musical process. Well, all of that ambition amounted to one night behind the mosh pit in a Jamaica, Queens, bar with a bassist-cum-Gunar Nelson look-alike.

But, one good thing emerged from that rebellious evening. I discovered that I could dance. Amongst the big-haired girls, and bigger-haired guys, I came to realize an innate musical talent I'd always had. I started rehashing my fancy-footed past. I had taken lessons, involving the memorization of routines to such tunes as Shirley Temple's, "Good Ship Lollipop" in all of the genres—tap, jazz and ballet. I owned all of the necessary footwear. At one time, I had amassed quite an extensive collection of Danskins. I had performed at recitals in green sequined leotards and feathered headpieces. I had choreographed an entire routine to "Oh Mickey You're So Fine," which I had debuted at Passover in front of the most critical of judges—my family. Years later, I had become obsessed with the soundtrack from Olivia Newton John's movie, *Xanadu*—at which point roller skates and leg warmers became part of my act. And, how could I have forgotten the roller rink, Laces, where I'd disco-skated to Michael Jackson, and break-danced with the boys?

Remembering my dance history, it all began to make sense. I was born to be a dancer! Suddenly, I was overwhelmed by the obviousness of it all. I, Daniella Brodsky, had always embraced music through dance. The body is my instrument, I realized.

And, I held to this idea all through high school, college and for years afterward. When my friends and I would hit the clubs and dance spots around the city, I would privately take pleasure from the inferior dancers that surrounded me. I took pride in being part of the Rhythm Nation. I went to Sapphire, Eau, Madison's, Guernica—anywhere and everywhere to strut my stuff to hip-hop, house, R&B and dance classics. I wore form-fitting clothing that would give and show skin at just the right moments to enhance a twirl, a hand gesture, a soft caress to a hip, an arm, a leg. I mastered the art of dancing in teetering heels. As other parts of my life peaked and plateaued, I took comfort in this one constant.

But recently, a friendship I'd developed with a neighbor reached a new plateau. He called it honesty. I called it the end of an era. It happened at Opal. We'd spoken a great deal about my love of dance, so when we happened to walk by this bar, fitted with a dance floor in back, he suggested we stop in (he was very sweet that way). After a couple of drinks, we found a good spot near the DJ and started grooving. Only he got very silent, and smiled way more than usual. When I asked him what the matter was, he'd paused for a second, but then said, "nothing." So I chalked it up to him feeling a bit inferior on the dance floor and let it slide. I'd encountered this before. I knew it was best not to bring it up. People are very sensitive about their dancing.

It wasn't until weeks later that the problem began to surface. We were playing that game Truth or Dare with a bunch of his friends. It was his turn. In lieu of running down the hallway naked, he opted for the truth alternative. Since I was the newest person in the group, the following was posed to him: "Tell us something about Daniella that we don't know." I figured he'd tell them I was a closet *Once and Again* watcher, or that I'd recently been 35 pounds heavier. But, I never could have imagined what he'd actually come out with: "She's not nearly as good of a dancer as she thinks she is. In fact, on a scale of one to ten, I would give her a three."

Now, in my friend's defense, I'd have to add that he'd drunk quite a few Twistinis I'd concocted that evening. And although the end result is really the same, he hadn't meant to say that out loud. Everyone laughed and insisted I set the record straight by performing atop the coffee table. And, in my intoxicated state, I figured this was a good idea. After all, I'd had so many successful dancing years, my friend's negative opinion was surely a product of bad taste on his end. I mean, I was almost embarrassed dancing with *him* on the night in question.

We were very professional about the whole thing. I selected "Say My Name" from Destiny's Child, and everyone was handed a blank sheet of paper and a Sharpie, with which to write their scores. It was all very *Dance Fever*. My "friend" introduced me, emcee-style to thunderous applause. He turned the lights down low and the stereo up high. I incorporated all of my best moves. I kept my eyes shut to avoid embarrassment.

When, breathless and full of anticipation, I finished my routine, the votes were cast. Of the eight participants, only one rated me higher than a 2.5. I'm sure I don't have to tell you how devastated I was at these most unexpected findings. The following weeks consisted mainly of MTV video viewing, accompanied by in-depth dance analysis. I wrote letters to all of the greats, J-Lo, Madonna, Britney, even Paula Abdul, seeking advice. But, hence, I received no answers, found no solace. For months, I would not hit the dancing scene with my friends.

Some time later, when my closest friend insisted I make a comeback "and stop acting like a child," I acquiesced. But, rather than step one foot on the dance floor, I hung close to the DJ booth, and found myself explaining my whole dilemma to the resident spinner. He was more than helpful. He suggested I try my bout at spinning the music, rather than trying to move to it. I entertained the thought for a few moments, until he whispered to me that he, himself, had never had any moves to speak of; dancing moves, that is. But, he did have some other sorts of moves, and did I mind if he tried them on me? Well, I hadn't minded one bit (being that he was adorable), so overlooking the DJ Rule (this is an entirely different situation, I reasoned), I allowed myself to be pursued by the adorable DJ. Maybe, I thought, there's a muse in me yet.

Viva Variety

If there's one thing New York is infamous for, it's abundance of choice to satiate our ever-insatiable search for entertainment. We've got two major league baseball teams, two minor league baseball teams, countless coastal destinations to dash off to, and just about every type of cuisine under the sun (in addition to new varieties, that fuse each of those with each of the others), and God knows what else. So, in the nightlife arena, when the time comes that swank scenes, traditional pubs and pick-up establishments leave a sour taste in your mouth, you'll need to step away from the ordinary (if only for a night), in search of something beyond the norm. In New York City a drink can be enjoyed while participating in almost any pastime, be it arcade games, bowling, billiards or dancing on the top of a bar (with or without a bra). Looking for something new? Read on.

ECLECTIC ACTIVITIES AND ENTERTAINMENT

Sure you've played pool at a bar, maybe even a video game or two, but the spots listed here take those otherwise ordinary pastimes to new heights, and for those who'd rather watch the entertainment than partake in it, perhaps a drag queen show or a belly dancing performance may be more up your alley.

BAR CODE

1540 Broadway (btw. 45th & 46th) Midtown West 212-869-9397

Everyone needs a bit of over-stimulation once in a while, which is why people head to Las Vegas every once and again. In the middle of our own Disneyfied Las Vegas Blvd., Times Square, you'll find BAR CODE, where video games and every sort of electronic pastime are at your disposal. *Cosmos cost $12. Bartender's Pick: Red Crush Cocktail made with Bacardi 8, triple sec, cranberry and orange juices and grenadine, over crushed ice ($9). Kitchen open Mon.-Sun. 11am-2am. Appetizers: $5.95-$12.95, entrees: $8.95-$10.95. Happy hour Mon.-Fri. from 11am-7pm means $4 premium well drinks, $2 domestic bottles and $1 domestic drafts.*

Bowlmor Lanes

110 University Pl. (12th & 13th Sts.) West Village 212-255-8188

Only in New York would you find a bowling alley with an attended elevator, a place where over-worked city-dwellers turn the No. 1 suburban pastime into something cool. Companies and organizations have parties here all the time, so Bowlmor is always packed with a variety of people. Mondays from 10pm-4am, come for Night Strike, where $20 gets you unlimited glow-in-the-dark bowling, to the tunes of DJs spinning house and techno. Want a nosh? A step above bowling alley fare, Bowlmor serves burgers and more sophisticated eats (from $5.50-$15). *Mon.-Thurs. after 5pm $6.95 per person per game, Fri.-Sun. and holidays $6.95 per person, per game. Shoe rental $4.00.*

Lucky Cheng's

24 1st Ave. (btw. 1st and 2nd Aves.) East Village 212-473-0516

What's life without a little dose of drag queen entertainment? Lucky Cheng's is nothing if not innovative, from its shoe-cum-dessert platter, to its crazy cabaret acts that thrive on audience participation (and humiliation), to its karaoke bar, to its downright gaudy interior. *Cosmos cost about $8. Bartender's Pick: Lucky Cheng Margarita jazzed up with a bit of Grand Marnier ($8). Shows performed Mon.-Thurs. 8:30pm, Fri.-Sat. 7:30pm and 11pm in the restaurant. $15 food minimum per person, and reservations are suggested 1 wk. in advance. Kitchen open Mon.-Fri. until 10pm, 12am on Sat. Downstairs, karaoke costs $3 Mon.-Fri. and $5 Sat.-Sun.*

Le Souk

47 Ave. B (btw. 3rd & 4th Aves.) East Village 212-777-5454

After a night watching the male belly dancers at this French-Moroccan restaurant, you'll wonder why there aren't more spots featuring this type of entertainment—it's such a great way to pass an evening. They also offer diversions of other varieties, like hookah pipes to add to your fun ($13 for an apple hookah for half an hour). All year long, retreat to the Moroccan tent out back. Call about belly dancer performances (days subject to change). *Cosmos cost $7. Bartender's Pick: Guavatini made with vodka, triple sec, guava juice and sloe gin ($7). Kitchen open Sun.-Thurs. 6pm-12am, Fri.-Sat. 6pm-1am. Appetizers: $6-$7, entrees: $14-$16.*

Pressure/(above Bolwmor Lanes)

110 University Pl. (12th and 13th Sts.) West Village 212-255-8188

If you've spent any amount of time on University Place near 13th Street, you've doubtless noticed a tennis bubble over the building housing Bowlmor Lanes. But, look closely. It's not just a bubble. It's a rooftop phenomenon, which, despite its name, will cause you to feel weightless and miles away from earth. This bar/pool hall/private party space—took the spacey bubble theme and ran with it, filling the place with inflated works of art, cube-like furnishings, dramatic archways and tons of neon lights and psychedelic screens playing movies like The *Usual Suspects* and *Barbarella* right on top of each other (for a truly eerie effect). So, if you're busy at one of the 29 pool tables (per hour: $24 for 2 players; $28 for 3; $30 for 4), sitting by the bar, munching on appetizers like filet mingon skewers or shrimp tempura ($10-$17) or lounging on a velour chair, you may forget that you were waiting for a lane downstairs, or decide that you're just too comfy to descend down to earth. *Cosmos cost $10.50. Bartender's Pick: Watermelon Martini made with watermelon liquer, Grey Goose vodka, and a touch of vermouth ($10.50). Open Thurs.-Sat. from 7pm on.*

Slate

54 West 21st Street (bet. 5th and 6th Aves.) Chelsea 212-989-0096

Where else can you buy an $800 bottle of Herradura Suprema, play pool or snooker, lounge out in high style, have a meal and listen to a DJ while watching a sporting event on the telly? Slate, formerly known as Chelsea Bar and Billiards, houses 40 pool tables, a restaurant offering a full Mediterranean-inspired menu (appetizers like crisp feta cheese sticks with olive tapanade are delightful), two bars, two lounges and a private party room. And, if you hadn't already caught on, this is no average pool hall. Sticks are stashed in Martha Stewart-style metal bins, blue lights spill over the main floor (you'll find more tables and a second bar downstairs) and a mile-long bar is made from layers of cracked glass, illuminated with alternating colored lights. So, pop in *The Color Of Money* for a bit of inspiration and head over for a couple of games ($14 per hour on weekends, $12 weeknights) and down a cool cue cocktail like the Corner Pocket or the Blue Chalk ($10). *Cosmos cost $10. Bartender's Pick: Sneaky Pete made with banana, coconut, and pineapple rums, lime and orange juices and 151 ($10). Open Mon.-Sun. 11am-4am. Kitchen open Mon.-Thurs. 11am-2am, Fri.-Sun. 11am-3am. Appetizers: $6-$10, entrees: $10-$15.*

Hurry Date by Shecky's

Log onto Sheckys.com and sign up for their e-mailing list to find out about the next Hurry Date event. At various bars around the city, 50 men and 50 women are granted 3-minute hurry dates with opposite-sex participants to find out if they are real-date-worthy. While the process may seem nutty and nerve wracking, after the first few Hurry Dates (and all-you-can-drink cocktails, included with the $24 fee), it's actually a lot of fun, and quite pressure-free.

Morning After Ritual #2: Be a bookworm

It's a well-known fact that women read a lot more than men (gosh, aren't we just so much more evolved?). Whether you're looking for a bubble-gum romance, a trashy back issue of *Cosmo*, a 1980 edition of *Vogue* or a heart-wrencher from those infamous Brontës, here're some of the best places to browse:

Barnes & Noble The intellectual's equivalent of the pick-up bar. And the best part? There's one on just about every other block. Browse the new titles, piss off the salespeople by sitting on the floor, and find yourself about ten books. Read them over a machiatto and don't buy any of them...except this one, of course.

There are stores throughout Manhattan in all your favorite neighborhoods including Greenwich Village, Union Square, Lincoln Center and the Upper East Side. All branches are open everyday. Check for hours.

Gallagher's Design, advertising and magazine industry insiders rely on Gallagher's collection of back-issue and vintage magazines for inspiration. Just remember: this is not a library, and the staff will make sure you understand that. Purchase your retro glossies and head somewhere to laugh, learn or wonder about times past.

126 E. 12th St. (btw. 3rd and 4th Aves.), 212-473-2404, open Sat. 12-6, Mon.-Fri. 9-6:30.

Partners & Crime

Got a soft spot for mysteries? Find current, out-of-print and first-edition chillers, thrillers and spine-tinglers here. Grab a seat on the sofas or chairs around the shop and enjoy. On the first Saturday of each month (at 6pm and again at 8pm) come for 40's-inspired mystery radio show performances.

44 Greenwich Ave. (at the foot of Charles St./btw. 6th and 7th Aves.), 212-243-0440, open Fri and Sat. 12pm-10pm, Sun. 12pm-7pm, Mon.-Thurs. 12pm-9pm.

Bluestockings

This is a bookshop just for us women! Almost all of the books, both fiction and non-fiction are penned by females and span lots of categories, from classics to modern novels as well as women's studies, parenting, lesbian literature, and health. Lounging out is encouraged, and coffee and desserts are available. Ask about events like open-mike nights, author readings, and women-of-color round tables.

172 Allen St. (btw. Stanton and Rivington Sts.), 212-777-6028, open Tue.-Sat. 12pm-8pm, Sun. and Mon. 12pm-6pm.

Strand Bookstore

You could very easily spend an entire day sifting through the topics in the eight miles of books in this dusty, labyrinthine shop. Scan new and old paperbacks and hardcovers in all categories from art to history to fiction, at seriously discounted prices (most about 50% off). Check the bargain shelves outside for books as cheap as a dollar.

828 Broadway (at 12th St.), 212-473-1452, open Mon.-Sat. 9:30am-10:30pm, Sun. 11am-10:30pm.

MUSICAL MEANDERINGS

When was the last time you dedicated an evening to live music? Whatever your passion, be it classics or new music, from well-known, unknown, or soon-to-be-known acts—you couldn't be in a better city to indulge.

Arlene Grocery

95 Stanton St. (Ludlow & Orchard Sts.)
Lower East Side 212-358-1633

Lots of fantastic bands play at this tiny former bodega turned hole-in-the-wall music venue. Groupies and band devotees come to watch their favorite groups play nightly. When a popular act is scheduled, come early, or you'll wind up sitting on the floor (which is far from sanitary), or standing smooshed between barstools or other latecomers forced to stand. Recently, they've added booths for a bit of a comfier environment, but early birds will still fare the best. Because of the variety of acts that grace Arlene Grocery's stage, the crowd is an eclectic one. Fri.-Sun. there's a $5 cover (and periodically for certain bands during the week), with five to six bands playing nightly, beginning at 7pm. Drinks range from $5-8. Check the schedule of events at the website: www.arlene.grocery.com. *Cosmos cost $8. Bartender's Pick: Cherry Bomb made with a very strong secret recipe ($8).*

Baggot Inn

82 W. 3rd St. (btw. Thompson and Sullivan Sts.)
West Village 212-477-0622

This music venue is normally packed with groupies and friends of, which means the crowd changes with every act. The décor is kept simple: black. Door price is normally about $5 for shows, which start at 7 or 8pm (check their calendar at the bar). There is no cover on Wed. for the bluegrass music jam, or Tues. for blues night. Stop in for happy hour everyday from 11am-7pm for $3 select cocktails and $1.50 mugs of Bud or Miller Light. *Cosmos cost $6. Bartender's Pick: White Chocolate Raspberry Martini made with Stoli Raspberry and Godiva white chocolate liqueur ($6.50).*

Continental

25 3rd Ave. (at St. Mark's Pl.) East Village 212-529-6924

Yes, there really is still a portion of the male population who thrive on looking like members of Poison. And they raise their glasses here. The walls are lined with photos of rock legends and the stage is graced with bands of the rock, punk and heavy metal persuasions. But, serious grunge dictates that you pack some tissues and hand sanitizer for a trip to the ladies room. *Cosmos can be made on the rocks (you'll probably get a funny look though) for $6.50. Bartender's Pick: 5 shots of anything for $10. Drinks are half price from 4pm-8pm. Minimum of three bands per night, every night (from 8:30pm weeknights, 9:30pm weekends). Cover for some bands ($5-15).*

Culture Club

179 Varick St. (King & Charlton Sts.) SoHo 212-243-1999

Although Culture Club's retro scene seems to be a favorite of tourists, commuters and the lingering-longer-than-most after-work set, the power of re-living the glory days can be just as cleansing as, say, a colonic. The telltale DeLorean evokes a simpler era where gummy bracelets and lacey ankle socks were de rigueur. Prepare for a musical feast featuring the likes of Madonna, Michael Jackson and Wham! A girl's got to reminisce. *Cosmos cost $5-$7. Bartender's Pick: Purple Rain made with Bacardi Limon, grape kool aid and sour mix ($9). Call for reduced admission before 8:30pm the night of—or farther in advance if possible. Regular admission $20.*

Duplex

61 Christopher St. (at 7th Ave.) West Village 212-255-5438

When overcome by the desire to escape ex-dot-com-ers and Wall Street duds, mix with the predominantly gay crowd at Duplex. The street-level piano bar lures performers and singing waitresses with personality galore to inject life into a worn-out urban populace via show-tune extravaganzas. Patrons sing along, either at their tables or by the piano, and sometimes render surprisingly moving solos. When the staff feels like enforcing the rule, you'll have to down the two-drink minimum, but you won't resent it. Time flies when you're belting out the best of Barbra. *Cosmos cost $7.50. Bartender's Pick: Scotch Drink made with 7 secret liquors, along the lines of a Long Island Iced Tea ($7.50). Feel free to order from their book of local delivery menus. Outside seating until 12am weeknights, 1am weekends until Oct. 30th. Check their calendars for cabaret acts in the 70-seat theatre; book in advance; tickets priced from $5-15 with a 2-drink minimum. Happy hour Mon.-Fri. 4pm-8pm means 2 for 1 beer, wine and well drinks.*

55 Bar

55 Christopher St. (6th and 7th Aves.) West Village 212-929-9883

Apparently free popcorn and first-rate jazz and blues acts are a winning combination. Which is why 55 Bar has not had to change its appearance, upgrade their bathrooms (too much), or stop enforcing the two-drink minimum in over three decades. Listening to talented performers sing and play their hearts out may be just what the doctor ordered. 55 Bar is a vestige of a West Village of yesteryear, free of trend, attitude and modernity. (I am told, though, that after recent structural repairs, bits of the ceiling no longer fall into your drink — they do apologize for the slight change). *Cosmos cost $6.50 during the day, $7.50 at night. Bartender's Pick: Stella Artois ($6). Mon., Wed., Thurs. 9:30 show is $15 including 2 drinks. Tue. show starts 9:30pm for $3 and 2-drink min. Fri.-Sat.: Early jazz show is free from 6pm-9:15pm, late blues show 10pm-2am about $5 with 2 drink min. Bar opens Mon.-Sat. at 1pm.*

The Cutting Room

19 W. 24th St. (Broadway and 6th Ave.) Chelsea 212-691-1900

No, it's not merely the place to go when Eugene's down the block isn't letting anyone in. With up-and-coming bands, and renowned musical and comedy acts like Sheryl Crow and Janeane Garofalo taking the stage, The Cutting Room has garnered quite a following. Best to reserve tickets in advance for big-name acts. Each night, you'll find three bands take the stage (ticket prices about $5-$10; more for bigger acts). On the menu: an eclectic mix of American and international cuisine, from tapas to pizza, to wrap sandwiches. *Cosmos cost $9. Bartender's Pick: Apple Martini ($10). Kitchen open Mon.-Thurs. 12pm-12am, Sat. 8pm-2am, closed Sun. Appetizers: $8-$11, entrees: $13-$18.*

Joe's Pub/(at the Public Theatre)

425 Lafayette St. (btw. E. 4th St. and Astor Pl.) 212-539-8777

Named for the late Joseph Papp, the Public's founder, this pub is actually a musical venue for top-notch acts ranging from Macey Grey to Duran Duran. Tickets range from $10-$40 and are available through Telecharge. The bar also hosts a happy hour from 6pm-about 8pm before shows, and re-opens at 11pm after performances for other musical acts and/or DJs for a $10 cover. *Cosmos cost $10. Bartender's Pick: Vanilla Shanti made with Stoli Vanilla, pineapple juice, fresh lime juice and Liquor 43 ($11). New Italian menu served Mon.-Sun. 6pm-1am. Appetizers: $5-$13, entrees: $13-$24.*

Music on Bleecker Street

Many a top-name act has gotten its start at a Bleecker Street bar. On the blocks between Sullivan Street and LaGuardia Place, you'll find cover bands that play the best of classic rock, and a mix of new tunes, in laid-back environs.

The Bitter End

147 Bleecker St. (at Thompson St.) 212-673-7030

For over 40 years, The Bitter End has been a venue for many musical headliners — recently bands like Rusted Root and Nine Days appeared here. *Rock, acoustic, jazz and heavy metal bands take the stage from 7:30pm-2am Mon.-Thurs. and 8:30pm-3:30am Fri.-Sat. Cover is about $5.*

Kenny's Castaways

157 Bleecker St. (btw. Thompson and Sullivan Sts.) 212-979-9762

Rock-and-Rollers play nightly, performing well-known cover tunes and a bit of their own stylings. *There are five bands on Sun, Wed., Thurs. and Fri. starting at 9:30pm, and six bands on Fri. and Sat. starting at 8pm, Mon. and Tue. are slower with 2-3 acts. Cover from time to time about $5.*

Red Lion

151 Bleecker St. (at Thompson St.) 212-260-9797

Remember when you would live and die for rock-and-roll? Well, sometimes it's nice to get back to that state of mind. Listen to cover bands play anything from Led Zeppelin to Eric Clapton. Sing along. Order up some appetizers and reminisce about hanging out in the parking lot/7Eleven/woods/schoolyard. *Shows run Mon.-Sun. 7pm-4am. Most nights are classic rock, Wed. is funk, Sun. is blues. Cover Sun.-Wed. $3, Thurs.-Sat. $5.*

Terra Blues

149 Bleecker St. (btw. Thompson St. and LaGuardia Pl.) 212-777-7776

Live musical acts everyday of the week. *Acoustic solo guitarists at 7pm, electric blues bands at 10pm. $5-$10 cover after 9pm. 2 drink minimum per person, per set.*

Celestial Bar Guide

Can't decide where to go? Look to the stars. But to find the bars listed here, look to the index.

Aries (March 21 - April 20): You're the Beyoncé of the group, a natural leader. Your pals depend on you to find the perfect spot more often than you'd probably like. But, the great thing is holding the reins means you can feed your need to fly by the seat of your pants. Point the crew somewhere that adds a dose of flavor to an otherwise fat-free scene. Try a Latin club like the **Copacabana** for salsa dancing, or take the crew to **Barcode** for some game playing.

Taurus (April 21 - May 21): A closet Jane Austen-type, you love to imagine yourself in dreamy environs. Bring romance novels off the page and into your life—head to **Chez Es Saada**. Perhaps your prince charming will show up. Perhaps not. Either way, you organized types will have the days leading up to your excursion to dream up a great saga (which is the best part anyway).

Gemini (May 22 - June 21): While your easy-going nature means you make the best of any place you happen to be dragged to, you'll have the best time where you can mingle to your heart's content. Head to a crowded happy-hour spot like **Joshua Tree** where you're likely to strike up a few conversations, to say the least.

Cancer (June 22 - July 23): Getting you to consider Saturday night as anything other than Blockbuster Night is difficult enough. Crowds, lines and ogling boys will send you right into hibernation. So, opt for a peaceful boite like **No. 9**, where you can sip your drink in serenity.

Leo (July 24 - Aug 23): Anything of the chill-out variety is definitely not up your ally, lioness. Seek stimulation at a place where anything can happen. **Hogs n' Heifers** is a wild spot, but a great dancing scene like **Nell**'s is also a safe bet.

Virgo (Aug 24 - Sept 23): A spot that's BYOTP (Bring Your Own Toilet Paper) will have you out the door before you can say "Cosmo please." For a super-clean WC and a beautiful space all-around, check out **Underbar** at the **W Union Square** or **Tja!**.

Libra (Sept 24 - Oct 23): You worship at the altar of fashion, and follow the gospel according to *Vogue*, so you need a swank destination to show off all that style, because, daahling, that to-die-for DVF wrap won't do you any good if it's hanging in your closet. You'll need to shimmy over to **Lotus** where your couture will work you through the velvet ropes.

Scorpio (Oct 24 - Nov 22): The pick-up scene is not your thing, to say the least. So, head to a spot where you can sit with your friends and enjoy a pitcher of sangria and a great order of moules frites. **Café Noir** is the perfect choice.

Sagittarius (Nov 23 - Dec 22): When the temperature rises, move the party outdoors. You'll feel like you've escaped the confines of the city (if only for a night). And who knows, if you have enough rum drinks, you may be able to convince yourself that you're at a seaside bar in St. Martin. A few to try: **Bot**, **Bowery Bar**, **Bryant Park Grill**.

Capricorn (Dec 23 - Jan 20): You work so hard—playtime needs to be rewarding. You need a place where you can really unwind (without spending a lot of cash). Good, cheap grub and $2 beers make **Reservoir** a good-time bargain. You won't need to spend hours getting ready and since you like to dress the part—just shimmy into a pair of blue jeans, skip the stilettos and cue up for a game of pool.

Aquarius (Jan 21 - Feb 19): It's not likely that you give a rat's ass where Leo or Madonna choose to down their cocktails. But the varied group you run with assures that you get exposed to many different scenes (some you'd rather skip). For a no-tude watering hole that won't leave you or the group snoozing, try: **Black and White**.

Pisces (Feb 20 - March 20): Wake up from that daydream and realize that just because you're going out, doesn't assure that you will meet Mr. Wonderful this evening. Just concentrate on having fun. If you haven't been to **The Park**, you just may find it's the perfect spot.

As a child, you were told not to play with your food. But now you're an adult, so you can do whatever you want.

Artisanal

2 Park Ave. (32nd and 33rd Sts.) Murray Hill 212-725-8585

Don't be timid. Don't be turned off by the smell. This fromagerie/restaurant will make a cheese expert of you yet. They know you don't know your Gouda from your Gorgonzola. They won't laugh. Instead, they'll school you, help you expand your taste range, and send you home with a cheat sheet, too. And they'll gladly help you choose the perfect wine from their extensive collection to complement your cheese selections. (Just don't attempt to try them all in one night.) After a Fromagerie experience, you'll go home wiser, drunker, and with your top pants button undone. You'll swear off eating for a week. You'll call your gals and arrange another visit. You'll begin classifying your life with phrases like "pre-fondue" and "post-fondue." *Cosmos cost $12. Bartender's Pick: They wouldn't dare pick for you, but they will help you choose the very best wine to suit your tastes, from their selection of 170 available by the glass. Lunch served Mon.-Sat. 11:30am-3pm, dinner Mon.-Sat. 5pm-12am, Sun. 5pm-10:30pm. Reservations are suggested, or you can wait for a table at the bar.*

Tortilla Flats

767 Washington St. (at W. 12th St.) West Village 212-243-1053

Innovative at its opening in 1983, Tortilla Flats is proof positive that even the models and fashion industry folk in the West Village like to let their hair down once and again, and again. The famous bingo games are held on Mondays and Tuesdays after 7pm, with the esteemed prize of a tee-shirt and more importantly — a round of shots for your table. Mondays are a bit more cut-throat, with a Survivor rule that allows players to be "voted out of the game." Wednesday is Hoola Hoop/Las Vegas night where you can flaunt that skill you probably never thought you'd ever use again. In February, you can even win a prize for looking like Ernest Borgnine (Karen Duffy and Chris Farley were past winners). *Cosmos cost $6. Bartender's Pick: Margarita (about $8, depending on which of the 11 tequilas you'd like). Kitchen open Mon.-Sun. 12pm-12am. Appetizers: $2.95-$6.95, entrees: $7.25-$13, lunch menu features lower prices. Happy hour Mon.-Sun. 4pm-7pm means $5 off pitchers of margaritas and $2 Rolling Rocks.*

I AM WOMAN

Sometimes you really want to strut your stuff. No inhibitions allowed at these downright rowdy bars.

Coyote Ugly Saloon

153 1st Ave. (btw. 9th and 10th Sts.) East Village 212-477-4431

Way before the movie immortalized this bar, women were getting in touch with their inner exhibitionists and dancing on the bar, tossing their bras and getting downright drunk at this hole-in-the-wall. Needless to say, it is a favorite with men. *Cosmos are not served here. Whiskey and beer bar only. Bartender's Pick: shot of Jack and a beer ($9.50). Happy hour Mon.-Thurs. 4pm-7pm for two for one drinks.*

Hogs & Heifers

895 Washington St. (at 13th St.) West Village 212-929-0655

By now, everyone is well aware of this white-trash-chic, anything-goes Meatpacking District dive bar that lights up the night with its barrage of signs and multicolored string bulbs. It is not uncommon for drunk women to do some bar-top dancing, unhook their bras and attempt to ring it around the moose antlers for posterity (remember the Julia Roberts debacle?). Take-no-crap tap mistresses decked out in head-to-toe western attire are an inspiration to all women. Make sure you know what you want when you get up to the bar, or you will get an earful. And keep your hands off the bar, too. Every so often, the barmaids hop up to get jiggy with it themselves. *Don't order a cosmo here, the bartenders will give you a Pabst Blue Ribbon instead, and you'll like it ($1.75). Bartender's Pick: Whatever shot you're buying ($4.75-$7), "and you can buy me one too."*

Red Rock West Saloon

457 W. 17th St. (at 10th Ave.) Chelsea 212-366-5359

Chelsea's answer to those downtown dives-cum-crazy-drunk, shed-your-inhibitions, act-like-a-townie bars, Red Rock has all the attitude and options to let loose as those listed above. Enjoy! *Cosmos cost $7. Bartender's pick: Southern Comfort and lime ($5).*

KARAOKE

There's just something about alcohol that makes every girl think she's the next Alicia Keys. Well, whether you can belt it out with the best, or have the sort of voice that even your roommates ask you to keep to yourself, you can have your five minutes of fame at any of these bars' karaoke nights. And if the very mention of the word "karaoke" makes you think of the word "lame," take a moment of self-reflection. Is it really lame, or are you just chicken? Right—I thought you'd see yourself, microphone in hand, getting discovered by some undercover talent scout...

Asia Roma Restaurant & Bar

40 Mulberry St. (btw. Worth and Bayard Sts.) Chinatown

212-385-1133

True to its name, this Chinese eaterie is decorated with all the bamboo you could ever want. Karaoke starts at 7pm nightly.

Bourbon Street

407 Amsterdam Ave. (btw. 79th and 80th Sts.)
Upper West Side 212-721-1332

Just like the city where the famous street lies, Bourbon Street plays host to crazy nights with lots of liquor in all of its glory (which is probably why it was named No. 1 college bar by Citysearch.com for 2001). On Tuesdays, karaoke night runs from 10pm-2am. with $3 Bud and Bud Light bottles. Also, stop in on Ladies Night Wednesdays, where us gals get $1 frozen hurricanes and draft beers, $2 well drinks.

Fitzpatrick's

1641 2nd Ave. (Corner of 85th St.) Upper East Side
212-988-7141

A beautiful Irish pub, formerly part of the Waldorf Astoria, Fitzpatrick's hosts karaoke Sundays from 10pm-2am, with a company that goes by the name of Sexual Chocolate.

Nevada Smith's

(see page 79 for contact information)

Karaoke your heart out here Tuesday and Thursday nights from 7pm to closing.

Japas St. Mark's

11 St. Mark's Place (btw. 2nd and 3rd Aves.)
East Village 212-473-4264

If the very thought of stepping on stage gives you the jitters, you'll love Japas, where the wireless mike is passed around for would-be singers who'd rather just entertain themselves. Be prepared to spend some dough — there's a $20 drink minimum.

Planet Rose

219 Ave. A (btw. 13th and 14th Sts.) East Village 212-353-9500

Formerly a private club for Japanese businessmen, Planet Rose is now a household word among the hipsters. It's all karaoke, all the time (you actually have to pay $2 per song). Just put in a request, and watch the exhibitionist urge spread like wildfire. Japanese appetizers served all night ($5-$10). Plan your trip to Planet Rose for Tuesday's kitsch karaoke party, aptly named Pop Tarts, which hosts themed nights ranging from Motown to heavy metal, to inspire your wackier, tackier self, from 8pm-close ($5 cover).

Suite 16

(see page 148 for contact information)

Would-be singers with a yen for the fabulous can do their best to carry a tune at this posh spot on Monday nights.

When to go to Bay Ridge

When you're in one of those ruts where you're sure that walking naked across Washington Square Park wouldn't even raise a peep from the drug dealers, it's the perfect time to boost your self-esteem in Bay Ridge.

If you haven't already discovered this man goldmine, listen up. In a small Brooklyn neighborhood right by the Verrazano Bridge live more dark-haired men with rippling muscles and Armani Exchange shirts than in all of Cancun during spring break (remember how great that was?). And, the best part: you've already got an edge if your name isn't Antoinette and you work somewhere other than your father's bakery. It is not possible to go to any bar in this neighborhood without getting the attention of at least five good-looking guys named Tony or Vinny. Of course, these are not the kind of men you'll necessarily want to have a long-lasting relationship or meaningful conversation with, but you'll definitely want to feel what's going on under those tight gray shirts. And you can ride the wave of the ego-boost you'll get for at least a month, if not longer. A twenty-dollar cab ride shared with the ladies is a small price to pay to visit one of these hot spots:

The Salty Dog

7509 3rd Avenue (btw. 75th and 76th Sts.) 718-238-0030

This firehouse-inspired bar, all brick with an actual fire truck-cum-DJ booth, is wall-to-wall men on the weekends. You will most definitely have to weed through some zeros to find your heroes, but they are here. Just remember to pick your jaw up from the ground, because they don't make men like this in Manhattan. They do have old-fashioned ideas, and while that may cause problems in relationships, it works wonders for the courting. These men would never think of letting you pay for drinks, they will light your cigarette, and listen to everything you say about yourself as if you are truly one-of-a-kind. Feel free to dance as crazily as you'd like in the back area, or lounge on a barstool up front. Food is served until 10:30 when they clear the way for the dance floor. By the end of the night you'll wish you could just have some peace and quiet without everyone checking you out (I swear!).

Delia's

9224 3rd Avenue (Bet. 92nd and 93rd Sts.) 718-745-7999

One of the newer additions to the Bay Ridge scene, Delia's is just like a Manhattan lounge, with bordello-type red seating nooks, low lighting and ornate accessories. Low tables surrounded by armchairs do attract a certain amount of couples, but also seat large groups of guys who want to munch on their trendy hors d'oeuvres, like oysters on the half shell. "How you doin'?"

The Blue Zoo

8402 3rd Avenue (at 84th St.) 718-833-5414

Did you ever wonder what it would be like to sit at a table sipping the Don P's with Robert DeNiro and his crew in *Goodfellas*? Well, this is your chance to find out. Whether or not these guys are connected, they sure as hell act like they are. If you go to whip out your cash flow, you will only be reproached with cries of "Fuggeddaboudit." This lounge looks cosmopolitan with a wall-to-wall tropical fish tank behind the bar, jungle murals and leopard-spotted sofas. Certain nights offer live bands with cute musicians for your viewing pleasure.

Strike Out

A perfect time to search out a different type of scene is when you've got a date. Not that first date, where it's all candlelight and fine dining. Maybe not that second date, where it's all sexy lounge atmosphere and seduction scenes designed to get you out of your Diesel jeans and into something slinky from Victoria's Secret. So, suffice it to say I was on my third date with a guy who required constant stimulation just to stay awake. (Let's just say he had a mild case of Attention Deficit Disorder that resulted in his leaving pasta on the stove for three hours before remembering it had been put there in the first place.)

And, despite the fact that our first two dates had not followed the afore-mentioned traditional date pattern (our first was at a personal favorite restaurant of his that he was sure I would love—Pizzeria Uno; the second was in his living room, eating take-out chicken wings, while his roommate watched Howard Stern re-runs on cable, repeating the words, "Dude, you gotta check out her tits"), I was retaining hope and trying to find an activity that we would both enjoy, and that would possibly bring us closer together.

The idea came to me in a dream, as if straight from God's mouth—bowling. Sure, bowling. Bowlmor Lanes is just round the corner, which means I could easily persuade Mr. ADD to come up for a nightcap. I could wear a cute 50's type ensemble complete with button-down blouse tied above the navel and hipster jeans that would look good when I bent over. Road testing this type of outfit can be quite tricky. A word of advice: standing on a stool with your back to a mirror and bending over to look at your rear end between your legs may result in injury.

It was a Sunday night, there were plenty of lanes available (which is rarely the case at Bowlmor), so we were able to get right at it. But, I had forgotten how horribly unflattering bowling shoes can be. Another thing I forgot is how horrible I am at bowling. But, I thought, if you laugh at yourself, it's fine. But, then I realized, if others start laughing at you, it's just downright embarrassing. And, if your ball bounces into the next lane, it can also be rather rough on your pride. (And may involve injuries that bring upon lawsuits that I am not currently at liberty to discuss.)

As it turns out, he thought it was cute that I couldn't bowl. It gave him the opportunity to teach me to be a better bowler, a technique that involved standing very close behind me and putting his arms on mine. The bad news is he wasn't going to give up until I'd become a better bowler. The good news is that you can order a beer, which helps to pass the time. The bad news is, the more you drink, the worse you bowl. The good news is, the more we bowled, drank, bowled, the more couple-like we became. At a certain point, I stopped worrying about the bad bowling and began having fun. This did wonders for my bowling mojo. I made more than one strike before the evening was through. Before we knew it, it was 1am. As far as I could tell the date had been a success. He was a very sexy bowler. That is, if there is such a thing as a sexy bowler.

But, bowling, it appears, is a very tiring activity for some men. Mr. ADD had expended all of his energy on bowling, which meant that he had no energy left for much else. And, the "much else" was a big reason why the bowling had been endured in the first place. So, when we'd finally made our way back to my apartment, I ran straight to the bathroom to "slip into something more comfortable," as they say. And, just to dab a bit of blusher on that "v" of my neck, which makeup artist Jenni Lee had so emphasized. And, to re-moisturize my legs. And, a bit of cellulite cream never hurt anyone. And, a quick brushing could probably do my teeth some good. And then a little mouthwash for fresh breath. And, ahh. I was all ready for a romp. But the sexy bowler had other ideas. With the TV on Sports Center and the blanket pulled high under his chin, the sexy bowler was fast asleep.

Clubs*

New York City has one of the richest nightclub histories in the world. We all know about Studio 54. We've seen the movie and enjoyed the renaissance of "If You Could Read My Mind." We also know that that era is over. The trend of hitting a dance club has now been replaced by selling your soul to see the inside of the newest Meatpacking District hotspot, or struggling to find the latest shoebox-sized bar with undisclosed name and address. Go-go dancers have been replaced by martini lists. Mirrored disco balls have given way to minimalist décor.

But, despite the changes, some clubs still thrive, and many city-dwellers start their evenings at 4 or even 5am to hear the DJs of the moment spin their stuff. But, their stuff is not the stuff of mainstream appeal. Their stuff has names like "drum and bass," "heavy house," "trance" and "garage" that most of us would be hard-pressed to understand, much less know how to dance to. But many clubs have gone down in flames, or suffered bouts of closings and re-openings due to liquor and cabaret license difficulties. The crowds at the warehouse clubs and midtown clubs can be young (at a fair portion, you need only be 18 to get in) and tend to be a mix of bridge-and-tunnel types, tourists, and music-scene aficionados that would sell their souls to be next to a DJ like Danny Tenaglia.

Yes, that is one part of the club scene. But if the spirit of the dance moves you, there are a plethora of places that play other types of music—from Latin to hip-hop to reggae and disco classics (including some of the smaller rooms at the super clubs). Many clubs change their parties from week to week, though, so the trick is to call and check out information sources like Flyer magazine (available at most record shops), The Village Voice, and Time Out New York, which list each night's parties with details you need to know before investing in pricey cover charges. Also check out www.clubplanet.com, and www.energynyc.com and www.brooklynunderground.net for party information and guest lists, and don't forget to pick up flyers at shops like 8th Street Lab and Patricia Field's for reduced admission. One thing that has not changed, though, is that knowing someone on the inside is the best way to avoid lines and reduce your entrance fee.

There is a small, but distinct group of smaller, chicer (not exactly Lotus, but more appropriate for the martini set) clubs, described in this section that keep it simple and cater to a more sophisticated crowd that wants to dance, no 18-year-olds, goth parties, thank you.

No matter where you chose to get your freak on, expect to pay a hefty cover (up to $25), and a high price for drinks. All clubs close their alcohol bars at 4am, and many serve juices and energy drinks after that. To get inside, steer clear of wearing sneakers, casual jeans (although for women, jeans paired with heels are pretty much the nightlife uniform these days), and make sure your male friends dress up too.

CLUB PARTIES TO RELY ON

To make matters even simpler, here is a list of some of the best long-standing parties around:

Don Hill's

511 Greenwich St. (at Spring St.) SoHo 212-334-1390

Wednesday night: Röck Cändy, Steve Blush's heavy metal party, has been around forever. Starting at 9pm, bang your head to rock favorites like Motley Cru and Guns n' Roses. The Rock Candy band plays heavy metal cover tunes on the second Thursday of every month if you need more. **Thursday night**: Beaver — here's your chance to relive the 80's. Rock out from 11pm on. According to the club, this night is a celebrity favorite. **Saturday night**: Tiswas is a Mod British music bash, where you'll hear the likes of the Who and The Kinks, spun by DJ Nick Marc from 9pm. People at this party tend to dress the part. *Cover for all parties $10.*

The Roxy

18th Street (at 10th Ave.) Chelsea 212-645-5156

Formerly the famous 1810, The Roxy houses the largest wood dance floor in the city, which doubles as a rollerskating rink. **Wednesday nights** you can skate with real old-school skates to retro classics, 70's, 80's and 90's. **Saturday**, the only other night the club is always open to the public, Roxy hosts a gay party with rotating deep house DJ's. Call about Friday evening special events. *Cover varies up to $25. Most parties 21+.*

Pyramid

101 Ave. A (btw. 8th and 9th Sts.) East Village 212-228-4888

Remember the New Wave? Got a hankering for old-school Madonna? Re-live the glory days at 1984, Pyramid's Friday night soirée, from 10pm on. Call for other nightly events. *Cover $7. 21+.*

Fun

130 Madison St. (under the Manhattan Bridge)
Chinatown 212-964-0303

One of the city's newer clubs hosts all kinds of special events and hires DJs across all musical genres. **Every last Thursday of the month is La Leche**—a fusion of Latin alternative and nuskool. **The second Thursday of the month** is Click + Drag—a synergy of three interesting themes—technology, performance and fetish—previously held at the former club, Mother. *Open Mon.-Sun. Cover $8, or none. All parties 21+.*

S.O.B's (Sounds of Brazil)

204 Varick St. (btw. Houston and King Sts.)
West Village 212-243-4940

Picture the Caribbean in all its vibrance. No wallflowers allowed at this energetic club. Mondays Live Latin bands from 6:30pm, and dancing lesson from 7pm-8pm for $15-$20. Fridays it's free admission with dinner reservation for R&B from 6pm-11pm ($12-$15 without reservation); latenight live Caribbean band after that for about $20. Saturdays Brazilian bands play from 8pm for $20. First Thursday of every month the Indian party basement, Bhangra, features Indian technofun from 9pm for $15. *All parties 21+. Kitchen open 6pm-12pm Mon.-Sat. (some Sundays). Appetizers range from $7-$10, entrees: $16-$22. Reservations are strongly suggested.*

SUPER-SIZED

Here are the giants of the club scene.

Copacabana (as of Spring/Fall 2002)

560 W. 34th St. (at 11th Ave.) Midtown West 212-239-2672

After 61 years, the legendary Copacabana closed its doors in 2001. But, not to fret, a bigger (48,000-square-foot), better, space is scheduled to open in Spring/Fall 2002 with two rooms — one for "American" music like hip-hop, house, and alternative, and one for Latin music like Salsa and Merengue. Meanwhile, the Copa is keeping its spirit alive with Saturday night parties at Club Pulse (226 E. 54th St., btw. 2nd and 3rd Aves; 212-688-5577). *All parties 21+.*

Exit 2

610 west 56th street (btw. 10th and 11th Sts.)
Midtown West 212-582-8282

Formerly known as Carbon, then Exit, now Exit 2, this club is open on Tuesdays for Latin night with rotating DJs and bands (free from 6pm-8pm; $20 later, 21+). Fridays, resident DJ Tony Draper spins house, techno and mainstream music ($30 from 11pm, 18+); Jr. Vasquez takes the turntables on Saturdays at 11pm for his house party ($30, 21+). This club, complete with roof deck, can fit over 5000 people. The crowd here tends toward the younger range with bridge-and-tunnelers, ravers and club kids. *Cover $30 (guest list $20). Drinks start at $8.*

Limelight

47 W. 20th St. (entrance on 6th Ave.) Chelsea 212-807-7059

With Peter Gatien's recent sale of the Limelight, and the persistent rumors that the club's liquor license is in jeopardy, it's improbable that this landmark nightclub (which re-opened a couple of years back after its last closure) will make it to its 20th birthday. But, for the meanwhile, this labyrinthine ex-church makes for one of the most well-known clubs in the city, spinning mainly house and hip-hop. Expect lots of bridge-and-tunnelers, club kids on who-knows-what and a ton of tourists who've come to see what all of the talk is about. The uppermost point — the chapel —

is a good place to escape the madness and grab a seat. Take a look at the Gieger room, designed by artist HR Gieger (if there isn't an S&M party you're not allowed into because *your* clothing is inappropriate). Sunday: John Blair's gay party. *Open Fri.-Sun. Cover ranges from $15-$25. 18+.*

Soundfactory

681 W. 46th St. (btw. 11th and 12th Aves.)

Hell's Kitchen 212-489-0001

Guidos, Upper East Siders and Brooklynites unite at this four-floor mega-club. In addition to three dance floors, ample seating of the white leather variety abounds. The interior is done up in the industrial style, with rotating artwork all about the space. Frequenters can get their hands on key cards for the 700-person VIP room, recently opened with separate DJ, bar and coat check. The club is only open on Fridays and Saturdays, spinning mostly house, trance and hip-hop on the various floors. *Cover 25+. Fri. 18+, Sat. 21+.*

Tunnel

220 12th Ave. (entrance on 27th St.) Chelsea 212-695-4682

Tunnel hasn't changed its look much over the years (even with the closings and openings), and is one of those clubs that seems to have something for everyone—with eight rooms spinning all types of music. Sunday nights, come for hip-hop with Funk Master Flex, but bring your own men to avoid major groping, and make sure they stay with you (you can even go to the co-ed bathroom together). Fridays and Saturdays vary. Check out the Fuzzy Room designed by Kenny Sharf. The crowd is largely B&T. At press time, Tunnel was closed, but we do hope that it will re-open shortly (history is on its side). *Open Fri.-Sun. only. Cover $25 ($20 on list). All parties 18+.*

Webster Hall

125 E. 11th St. (btw. 3rd and 4th Aves.) East Village 212-343-1379

If you can deal with the tourists and the outer-borough scene, you'll be just fine, because Webster Hall is still one of the most beautiful clubs in the city, and caters to all musical tastes in its series of rooms—choose from hip-hop, Latin, techno, house, 70's and 80's music. Fridays and Saturdays the crowd fills this four-floor club to the brim. *Cover $30, $20 with pass. Open Fri.-Sat., and on occasion certain weeknights. No jeans, no sneakers.*

Vinyl

6 Hubert St. (entrance on Hudson St.) TriBeCa 212-343-1379

Who says you need alcohol to have a good time? Not the devoted crowd at Vinyl, that comes to hear Danny Tenaglia spin on Fridays, even though the club has no liquor license. One of the most eclectic parties around, Be Yourself, is true to its name — you'll find uptowners, downtowners, ravers — gay and straight — and just about anyone else you can think of at this bash of modern, tribalistic, garage and house music. There is no dress code and for a refreshing change, everyone is granted entrée for $20. Die-hards arrive late (that's after 4am). Stock up on I Love Danny tees in various stages of deconstruction and "Be Yourself" logo'd gear like halters, tanks, and boy shorts ($20-$30). Saturdays come for techno, trance and house ($25), and Sundays afternoons put weekend warriors to the test. *Open Wed., Fri.-Sun.*

Don't Mix With the Help

At first sight, DJs and bartenders may seem like ideal date material, behind their turn tables and taps, but closer inspection will show that this Wizard of Oz type power is all smoke and mirrors. Here're ten reasons why it's a lose-lose situation.

- **The DJ/bartender talks** to more women in one night than the average guy does in a year—you're just one in a million women doting on him.

- **There is a mystique** surrounding the DJ/bartender that makes him seem appear much more attractive/witty (and even caring and understanding—depending upon how many beverages you have consumed) than he probably is.

- **If you do date** the DJ/bartender and it doesn't work out, you've lost your hangout, and perhaps your free-drink hookup.

- **Girls tend to throw** themselves at the DJ/bartender; if you enter their place of business unexpectedly, you may see them speaking to other women and suffer painful bouts of jealousy.

- **When you see** the DJ/bartender, chances are you will both be drunk and oblivious to each other's true personalities.

- **If you do** enter into some sort of relationship with the DJ/bartender, his late hours will mean that he will never take you out on dates (no free dinners, cute couple-like activities like ice-skating or watching the sunset).

- **Because you will** be drinking so many free drinks, you will inevitably gain more weight.

- **No matter how** cool the DJ/bartender seems in his natural habitat he will seem infinitely less cool in other environments.

- **And, most importantly,** you will never be able to meet any other men in that bar!

CLUB CHIC

For a smaller, more sophisticated, post-college crowd, take those dancing feet to one of these downsized clubs.

Centro-Fly 45 west 21st St. (btw. 5th and 6th Aves.)

Flatiron 212-627-7770

Formerly the rock-and-roll venue Tramps, Centro-Fly is now very much part of the club scene, populated by industry execs, club regulars and hipsters alike. Resident spinners are known for their underground and hard-house stylings. *Open Wed.-Sat. at 10pm. Cover $15 and up. All parties 21+.*

Chaos

225 East Houston Street (at Essex St.)

Lower East Side 212-475-3200

Picture velvet couches, chandeliers and a colorful lit-up bar. Chaos is a far cry from this space's former identity—a goth nightclub known as the Bank. With a musical roster spanning from Euro house to R&B, there's something for everyone. Sunday hip-hop parties are popular, and pricier (about $30 for women, $40 for men). *Open Fri.-Sun. Call for events. Cover varies from about $20-$40. Tables are bottle service only; prices vary. All parties 21+.*

Filter 14

432 W 14th St. (at Washington St.)

West Village 212-366-5680

I thought I was pretty cool when I was given the password to get in with no cover on a Saturday night, but then I thought, password? The idea is ridiculous, given that Filter 14 is an unfinished pile of rubble with a labyrinth of unattractive rooms, but in their defense, the password does serve its purpose with large parties, to ensure each member of the group actually gets inside. With so many other great spots popping up, it would appear that longevity would require a bit more effort and a splash of uniqueness. Apparently, permist problems have prevented this so far. Friday is more of a music industry night with house music. Saturdays you'll find more dance-friendly tunes. *Open Tuesday-Saturday. Cover about $12.*

Hush

17 W. 19th street (at 5th Ave.) Flatiron 212-989-4874

Catering to a chicer crowd, Hush offers lots of musical variety for the more mainstream music tastes, like Latin, and hip-hop. *Open Mon.-Sat. Call for events listing. Cover varies up to $20. All parties 21+.*

Saci

135 W. 41st St. (btw. 6th Ave. and Broadway)

Midtown West 212-278-0988

Host to hot events like Fashion Week extravaganzas, Saci attracts the moneyed scenesters, rather than the typical club set. Here you'll find more mainstream music than at most clubs. Although nights do change depending on the parties being promoted, Fridays are normally house and progressive, and Saturdays are hip-hop and R&B. Call ahead to make sure. *Open Thurs.-Sat. 10pm-4am. Tables are first come, first serve with bottle minimums from $200-$1200 depending on night, location and number in party. All parties 21+.*

Spa

76 E. 13th St. (btw. 4th Ave. and Broadway)

East Village 212-677-5772

Among the most exclusive clubs in Manhattan, Spa is promoted as the club "for people who have arrived," whatever that means. While you might not buy the idea that Spa is geared towards the health-conscious lifestyle, it does serve up 25 selections of water and fresh juices. But, they also serve up tons of alcohol to the scenesters who consider Spa home away from home. The space is one of the most beautiful around, in that steel-and-glass industrial aesthetic, and therefore lots of press events and private parties are held here. Tuesday is hip-hop, Wednesday dance to R&B, Thursday is alternative, and Friday and Saturday come for classic house, disco and techno. *Cover is $20 weeknights, $25 weekends. Open 10pm-4am. Closed Sun. and Mon. All parties 21+.*

W. 8th

40 W 8th St. (6th Ave. and MacDougal St.) West Village
212-477-9333

Yes, that's right. Eighth Street, between MacDougal and 6th Avenue. Shoe row. If you ever pictured anything beside eight-inch platform sandals on this block, it probably wouldn't be a shwanky scene. If any nightlife establishment planted its roots on this strip, you'd most likely expect a spot where one can don those "shoes" that tourists scoop up by the dozen. You'd be expecting wrong. W8th is actually a pleasant surprise. This below-ground boite (courtesy of Vig and Tribe proprietors) is half club, half bar — two rooms, two worlds. It's a true hipster hangout — in other words sunglasses are de rigueur and that Chloe-esque top is…wait, actually Chloe — and grabbing a table means forking over serious cash for a bottle ($200 minimum), but saves you lots of money at the door if you reserve in advance (you and 10 friends enter for free, and a guest list allows additional buds $5 off the normal $15 charge). Who would have guessed? *Open Wed.- Sat. 10pm-4am.*

The World/(at WWF)

1501 Broadway (at 43rd St.) Midtown West 212-398-2563

But, what about the wrestling ring, you ask? Believe it or not, there is no ring at the WWF, so the Saturday night transformation into a house and hip-hop dance club is not as hard to believe as one might think. The World books popular guest DJs, and has garnered its fair share of media and celebrity attention since its opening. Hosting Derek Jeter's birthday bash probably didn't hurt. *Cover $25-$30. All parties 21+.*

MAINSTREAM CLUBS

Finding the right spot to get your groove on, if you're into mainstream dance music, can be difficult in Manhattan. I, for one, am a mega-fan of cheesy dance music, and don't mind mixing with a few guidos in exchange for my favorite tunes. At these spots, this is the price you'll have to pay. So, forsake your attitude, bring your own party and dedicate the night to dance at these clubs.

13

35 E. 13th St. (btw. Broadway and University Pl.)
East Village 212-979-6677

This club is best known for its Friday and Saturday night dance parties ($10), where DJ Cadet spins R&B, hip-hop, classics and reggae for an eclectic crowd that really wants to boogie. Unlike most clubs, drinks are reasonably priced. *In season, escape to the roof deck for some peace. Thursdays is 70's and 80's, Brit-pop and new wave (no cover). Tuesdays, come for live bands ($5), and Sundays is the 60's and 70's British mod and punk (no cover). All parties 21+.*

China Club

268 W. 47th St. (btw. Broadway and 8th Ave.)
Midtown West 212-398-3800

Although the roster of musical performers who have graced this Club's stage would have one think it's the place to be, one would be sadly mistaken to follow this train of thought very far. Just enjoy the hip-hop, house and classics spun most nights, and don't waste your time looking around for Bruce Willis. *Open Mon., Wed.-Sun. Cover $20 and up. Call for schedule. All parties 21+.*

Cheetah

12 W. 21st St. (btw. 5th and 6th Aves.) Flatiron 212-206-7770

So overdone it's actually funny, Cheetah is seriously cheesy — like the kind of cheesy you never really knew existed before. But, on the bright side, you can wear that hoochie skirt you never thought was quite right elsewhere, pull out those shoulder rolls and memorized N'Snyc choreography you've been working on, and not worry about making a fool of yourself. Choose from house or hip-hop rooms on most nights. *Most nights $20 cover. Monday hip-hop party $10 for women, $25 for men.*

Cream

246 Columbus Ave. (btw. 71st and 72nd Sts.)
Upper West Side 212-712-1666

An interior decorator's nightmare, Cream breaks all of the design rules — mixing contemporary with traditional, casual with formal — in its multitude of rooms, ranging from a Victorian decor, to an icy white room, to a red lava lounge, to a Tokyo-bamboo motif. But, somehow, it works. Apparently, you can get away with anything when you are one of the few places to dance on the Upper West Side. *Cover $20 Fri.-Sat. All parties 21+.*

Étoile

109 E. 56th St. (btw. Park and Lexington Aves.)
Midtown 212-750-5656

The name means star, but it's doubtful the French have changed the definition to mean "Guido haven for Upper East Side Girls." And, if that's what you're into, by all means, enjoy! While men may have a hard time getting into Étoile without a membership, knowing someone, or flashing Armani, women need only wear form-fitting garments to make it past the velvet rope. Opt against securing a table unless you feel like shelling out hundreds of dollars to buy a bottle of alcohol or to eat a far-from-fabulous meal. And, yes, the faux latticed windows do nod to The Sound of Music, the nude Indian-inspired paintings do seem out of place, and no, I have no idea why the floral-printed seats are decorated with shiny teal and pink pillows circa 1990 Long Island. *Cover $20. Open Thurs.-Sat. All parties 21+.*

Float

240 W. 52nd St. (btw. 8th Ave. and Broadway)

Midtown 212-581-0055

While the attitude at the door might have you think Float is one hot club, you would be sadly mistaken. Men in muscle shirts and women in too-tight Lycra dresses (yes, they're still wearing Lycra dresses) make up the clientele. An empty dance floor and non-descript décor don't do much to help matters at this small club. *Open Thurs.-Sun. Cover $20 and up. All parties 21+.*

Ohm

16 W. 22nd St. (btw. 5th and 6th Aves.) Flatiron 212-229-2000

Short for "Oh My God, I didn't realize there were still so many guidos"? It's truly amazing how many can fit into the two-floors of Ohm. Any club that hosts a Jdate party one night, and a trance/techno party the next is obviously trying to find itself. Most nights the music is varied enough between the two floors that you'll find something to suit your tastes. *Open Thurs.-Sat. Cover varies up to $20.*

Metronome

915 Broadway (at 21st St.) Flatiron 212-505-7400

Formerly Café Society, Metronome is a spacious mini-club, with a sophisticated art deco décor. Open most Friday and Saturday nights for hip-hop, reggae and house. Lots of private events are held at this club/Mediterranean restaurant/jazz venue, so call ahead to make sure it's free to the public. On the last Friday of every month, Metronome does its part for "thirtysomethings," by hosting a party for those 25 and over only, with wine and martini tastings. *Cover varies up to $20.*

Speeed

20 W. 39th St. (btw. 6th and 7th Aves.) Midtown 212-719-9867

Four floors and a roof deck, mainly devoted to hip-hop and R&B, Speeed does that midtown thing—attracting lots of tourists, young crowds and B&Ts, along with locals, and top-name DJs like Funkmaster Flex and Mister Cee and Ace. But, many complain that Saturday nights the club is extremely empty—even way into the wee hours. Thursday nights are free for ladies. *Cover varies up to $25. Open Thurs.-Sun. All parties 18+.*

ONE IN A MILLION

Some clubs defy all the rules and cross all clientele categories and stay hip, fun and attitude-free over time. Here, it's all about moving and grooving, and really not much else.

Nell's

246 W. 14th St. (btw. 7th and 8th Aves.) West Village 212-675-1567

Nell's is in a class all its own. With no attitude at the door or otherwise, this West Village institution is for serious dancers, and serious dancers alone. Fridays feature old-school dance music (from Michael Jackson to Madonna) upstairs and hip-hop, R&B and soul down, others range from Cuban Soul Thursdays to Open Mike Night Tuesdays. Another refreshing difference: the crowd is totally eclectic—it's doubtful you'll see more than one Louis Vuitton sling in a single night! *Cover varies up to $15. All parties 21+.*

Club Kid

I would never say I was much of a club kid. In fact, while fellow NYU students were out taking hits of E and swinging glow sticks around, I could be found in the study lounge reading some classic or another and asking the biology majors to shut the hell up so I could concentrate. Apparently I missed out. But, hey, I graduated right? I'm older now, and I was sure I could handle a night out at "the club," as my girlfriend Mimi (a serious club girl) refers to any place they happen to be hitting that evening. So, when she decided to induct me into the scene by way of "research," I was all for it. Would I have to wear those big pants? I asked her. Apparently this was a funny question. We decided I should dress like a big hoochie, just for the fun of it, and so we hit the Rainbow Shop for some Jerry Springer-inspired duds. What I came out with contained an excess of Lycra and just covered my ass and boobs (somewhat).

I allowed her to apply my makeup, which was dominated by sparkles and various shades of blue. The effect was, well, different. But then, we parted ways. You see, you cannot just start the night out at one of the "real" clubs (read: those that play music that makes you feel like you have gotten really old) if you are really going to do it right. What you have to do is go about your night and then head to the bar at about 5 am, when Danny Tenaglia starts spinning. I actually drank a Jolt before the night began. I made plans with some other friends to review some Upper East Side bars. In hindsight, that was perhaps a poor plan. I mean, a girl would like some attention now and again, but, "Ooh baby, are those things real?" and "Can I just get one quick touch?" was a bit more than I could really take.

I dragged three friends out that night, in hopes that at least one of them would stay out all night with me. I bought them shots, desperately trying to stir up some excitement. The result was Jeremy puking at the table. One down. Then Michael met some chickie dressed like a big slut (wait, I was dressed like a big slut too, why hadn't I met anyone?) and left me with the last person, Ben. Ben talked big about staying up all night and watching the sunrise. Ben described serious dance moves involving twirls and intricate clapping movements, which would give him instant John Travolta status at "the club." Ben was very clear about how many women "would be on his jock" when he busted out the moves. Ben was snoring at the booth when I came back from the bathroom ten minutes later. I put Ben in a cab and headed downtown to my apartment to wait out the rest of the hours before Club Time.

At 1:30am I was home, sitting on my couch in my hoochie outfit, watching a re-run of Sex and The City. I bought two beers (light) at the corner deli to keep myself in the party mode. After Carrie and Big had done it three times I was getting a bit groggy. So, I turned off the TV and put on some dance music I'd downloaded from the Internet. I started dancing in front of the mirror to check out my moves. I tried to master sensual hair upsweeps and suggestive caresses on my curves. I tested a couple of dancing faces to see which was the sexiest. I looked to make sure the shades were closed (I do have a reputation to uphold). Then I had the brilliant idea of turning on MTV to see if I could garner some new moves from Britney and company. But, in my big leopard platforms those moves were not so easy to perform. I had to give those gals some props. Mid slide-spin-hop-snap movement my ankle gave out. I was a heap of Lycra, skin, platforms and glittery makeup. I'd fallen and I couldn't get up.

So, I laid down right there on the floor. In my semi-drunken state, I noticed how cool the wood planks felt on my face. In my semi-drunken state, I noticed how funny my apartment looked from this angle. In my semi-drunken state, I didn't realize that my ankle didn't hurt anymore. In my semi-drunken state, I fell asleep. I had many dreams involving ringing telephones.

When I awoke, the ex-cast members of the Real World were having a ten-year reunion. When I looked in the mirror, my hair had taken on an interesting shape that miraculously defied the law of gravity. There were sparkly bits of glitter on every square inch of my face. There was eye shadow on my nose? My hoochie outfit had twisted its way around my waist like a belt. There was a light blinking away on my answering machine.

"Daniella, I guess you're not home yet, I'll call you on your cell. We're gonna have so much fun. Listening to Danny is a religious experience. Your life will never be the same." Beeeeeep.

"Daniella, I tried you on your cell phone. We are just about to leave. I'm sure you are making out with some over-aged frat boy at some seriously cheesy Upper East Side bar, but you've got work to do, darling. Call me soon." Beeeeeep.

"Dani, where are you? We just crossed over the bridge and we'll be at your apartment in about ten minutes. I'll call you when we get there." Beeeeeep.

"Dani, I'm standing outside your building, buzzing for like ten minutes. Where are you? Short of climbing up the fire escape, I'm not quite sure what to do here honey." Beeeeeep. "Memory Full."

I felt bad that I had missed Mimi, but I felt even worse knowing that I would have to go through the entire thing again—all in the name of research.

Land of the Fabulous

Before deciding upon what is cool, you'd be well served to consider how a place actually achieves top billing. In Gotham—fashion and magazine central—the tastemakers are designers, editors, and celebrities who receive invites to every opening under the sun. A friend of a friend asks a Sarah Jessica Parker or a Gisele Bundchen to grace their cushy velvet couches with their multi-million-dollar arses; a snapshot of them, baby Piper in hand, makes its way onto the society pages and voila, the new Lotus is born.

Satirized in numberless ways, by all of us jealous outsiders, the requirements for steering clear of velvet rope burn are getting increasingly more ridiculous. But even with the passwords, reservations, and key cards, the days leading up to a jaunt at a chichi boite are always a thrill—filled with the intricacies of wondering what to wear, who to ask and determining which straightening product will keep the frizz out the longest. But, as with most longed-for events, the reality rarely pans out in the way you may have hoped. If your name was not (inadvertently) left off the list, then you may have been snubbed for wearing your imitation Fendi baguette or for sporting last year's Celine. But, if all goes well and you make it through the unmarked/hidden doors unscathed, ask yourself, did you really have a good time?

If your answer is yes, it is indeed time that you surround yourself with fabulous people who can name-drop a corporate affiliation that will get you on a VIP list or through the doors for the next time around, because a business card bearing the words MTV, *Vanity Fair, Elite Models* or the like is the strongest currency in this town (apart from an American Express Black Card, of course). If you're feeling fabulous and up for the challenge, here are the most chichi of the chichi. Please note that cosmo prices and bartender's picks for coolest cocktail have been omitted from these reviews, since the very mention of the cosmo might incite the staffs at these spots to gasp and make proclamations like, "daaahling, that is so last year." The thought that such hotspots might pin themselves down to touting a drink that may be un-trendy by publication date is just too ghastly. And of course, as sticking to the rules of uniformity is just so unchic, we wouldn't dare ask these spots to stick to the same rules as everyone else—this includes cocktail prices—so just realize that drinks are expensive, a night like this is an investment (if you were wondering, put off paying the Con Ed bill first, since they hold out the longest before cutting off service).

APT

419 West 13th St. (btw. 9th Ave. and Washington St.) West Village
212-414-4245

According to launch-master Ray, who is one of the Jonathan Moore pack (Eugene, Lush, Bond Street, Indochine), the reservations-only policy was put into play so that patrons won't feel the pain of the APT door slamming in their faces. You don't have to be part of the fab pack to book a table, and you won't be slapped with any hefty bottle-purchasing rules either. The main level books up to 30 guests per evening (book at least two weeks in advance), leaving space for "regulars." The apartment theme is played out seamlessly, care of designer India Mahdavi (of Townhouse Hotel fame). Finding the building can be difficult, with only a buzzer and number marking the door. Once inside, the vestibule is not unlike any New York residence's—exposed brick and all. Those reservationless hopefuls can try their luck in the basement bar—done up with faux wood paneling and a long communal counter, and listen up to the original stylings of seven alternating spin-masters, while pondering how those ladies get their hands on such amazing tops and when exactly the bra went out of fashion.

Balthazar

80 Spring St. (btw. Broadway and Crosby St.) SoHo 212-965-1414

If you happen to fall into the modern-day gold-digger category, here's the bar for you. Everyone is rich. This is where rich people eat, drink and, next door, buy their bread. Balthazar's extensive wine list is not to be beat. Your waiter would probably kiss your pinky toe if you asked. In typical French style, this eatery has an open, bustling energy, packed in with diners and drinkers enjoying the best of the best.

Bungalow 8

515 W. 27th St. (btw. 10th and 11th Sts.) Chelsea

Even though there's no "Bungalow 8" sign out front, discerning this bar's locale is quite simple via the flashing neon that reads "No Vacancy." Hotel life. Ah. And if Bungalow 8 serves as any sort of indicator, owner Amy Sacco could probably open up a very successful hotel if she so chose. If there were sleeping quarters upstairs one would literally never have to leave. The concierge is available to fulfill any and every request that beautifab sorts may have. There are medical services available, shopping services, a menu of yummies that includes caviar, as well as the option to order from just about anyplace that delivers. There is even an overnight bag for sale, filled with all of the items necessary to prevent the "walk of shame." The velvet-rope brigade is sweet as pie, and the waitstaff truly understands the meaning of hospitality. While the entire point is to feel like you are *en vacances*, one does wonder just how many people actually take advantage of such shamefully indulgent services as those offered here.

Church Lounge/At the TriBeCa Grand Hotel

2 6th Ave. (at White St.) TriBeCa 212-519-6600

At its inception, this huge, loft-like space served as lounge, bar and restaurant to TriBeCa Grand hotel guests, and as a humbling experience to those New Yorkers who watched as those presumably more fabulous/important/connected-than-themselves passed the velvet rope, whilst pretending not to care. These days, entrée should be easier, as other coveted bars have opened up and taken their place on the list of most pretentious. A creative menu offers up everything from ravioli to filet mignon. And of course, you can down any new-and-cool-tini you'd like.

In Wait of the Ring

Don't sit staring at the cordless. The key to surviving the hours/days before "he" dials your digits is distraction. Although science has yet to produce a study on this ever-so-pertinent topic, it is a well-known fact that the best way to induce an eagerly awaited phone call is to leave your dwelling. Here are some ways to spend the time:

- **Go shopping!** Retail therapy is an excellent way to soothe the soul. And even if he hasn't phoned by the time you return, you've still got a new sweater/skirt/bauble to show for it.

- **Go out to eat** with your friends—if you can't talk to him, at least you can complain about it.

- **Hit the treadmill**—work out anger and burn calories, too.

- **Go to the movies**. But, avoid all plotlines involving dating, people who have dated, or people who could possibly date.

- **Spend time with** your family. After a day with relatives, it will be quite apparent that you have worse problems than this man-boy who still hasn't rung.

- **Visit an old friend.** Once you start babbling about all of the things going on in your life, you'll see that this un-received phone call is just a drop in the bucket.

- **Go out and meet someone else** (ultra-scientific study proves that when you turn your interests towards another, that original object of desire will undoubtedly turn his interest towards you).

Pangaea

417 Lafayette St. (btw. 4th Ave. and Astor Pl.) East Village 212-353-2992

One of the newest editions to the fabulous scene, Pangaea's owners have a swank history with spots like Spy Bar and Merc Bar, and therefore it's less shocking to find that they already admit to turning away up to 1,000 hopeful entrants a night. Those lucky enough to pass through will enter into a candle-lit mystical wonderland of Survivor-chic, underneath an elegant tent of draped material, embellished with tribal masks, spears, bows and arrows, and lots of pillow-topped couches. Although the crowd is kept to a minimum at opening (8:30pm), by midnight, it's wall-to-wall glamorous folk, ordering up champagne from the extensive collection, or house cocktails like the Jungle Fever, or the Pangaea Tribal—so sweet and smooth, you'll go through your non-recession-friendly-priced glass before you know it. A selection of appetizers and sushi are available at the teeny tables (which cannot be reserved in advance, and require bottle service), and if you're lucky, you can grab one near the drummers, who beat along to the house tunes spun nightly.

Grand Bar/At the SoHo Grand Hotel

310 W. Broadway, 2nd Fl.oor (at Grand St.) SoHo 212-965-3000

It is a pleasure to find that some spots can retain their panache and glamour even after the Page Sixers have come and gone. After five years, Grand Bar is still a comfortable, attitude-free (albeit pricey) destination. Whether you're planning a quiet weeknight meeting, or looking for a bustling weekend place, you can't go wrong. Get intimate in the lounge, or have a seat at the bar or tables opposite, order up some scene cuisine described with adjectives like "wrapped" and "braised," and see if any European tourists suit your fancy. Since the hotel is dog-friendly, don't be surprised if a little pooch makes an appearance. Recently, the bar has been promoting its listening sessions with new lounge records from 6pm-7pm nightly, and DJ sessions with everything from drum and bass to break beats (Mon. and Thurs. 8pm-12am, Fri. 10pm-12am).

Halo

49 Grove St. (btw. 7th Ave. and Bleecker St.) West Village 212-243-8885

Any bar that hosts J-Lo's birthday bash on its opening night has a right to have a bit of a 'tude. But, anyone who's been denied entrance to Halo will concur that the restaurant/bar/lounge may in fact be in need of an attitude adjustment. Inside sources admit that gaining entrée can be difficult, if not impossible late nights. For a guarantee, head over early (about 10pm) or make a reservation for dinner. Those that make it in no problem (models, celebs, friends of, media) will rave. The specialty drinks, like Tropicaltini, Apple Martini, Chocolate Martini are served in oversize martini glasses and pack a punch. Hold on tight, though, because after midnight, the downstairs space is so crowded that pushing and shoving are survival tactics that people don't feel the need to apologize for. Thursday nights DJ Jus-Ske spins hip-hop and 80's tunes for one of the best parties, but weekends are always packed too—with some of the most beautiful men and women you've ever seen.

The Hudson Bar at the Hudson Hotel

356 W 58th St. (btw. 8th and 9th Aves.) Midtown West 212-554-6343

Ascend the endless escalator up the stairs to the Hudson Hotel's lobby, where foliage is plentiful, and make a right. If you're a hotel guest or on the list, you're good to go, otherwise you'll have to do your best convincing with the door staff. Rejectees (don't get depressed since 90 percent of us would fall into that category) can try the rooftop Park Bar when the weather's right—and this is no comedown, since the space is beautiful, with café tables and lots of flora to boot. If you do have a well-connected friend/friend of a friend/business associate with favor due, you'll find Hudson Bar is sleek and sexy all the way with lots of white leather, elegant tables and lighting low enough to hide any period pimple that may have popped up. Up above, a painting described to me as "a self portrait of the artist with everything sprouting from his penis," can serve as a wonderful conversation piece with just about any guy. Although the Hudson Bar has a multicolor, light-up dance floor, I did not see a single too-skinny, too-beautiful, but (oh, where did she get that purse?) blonde shaking her thang.

Hudson Library Bar

356 W. 58th St. (btw. 8th and 9th Aves.)

Midtown West 212-554-6317

It's reservations only at this quiet, swanky book-lined lounge, where VP-types and the fashion set get away from it all. Shoot a rack at the purple pool table, underneath one enormous lighting fixture, try your hand at chess, or just inspect the black and white hatted-cattle photos, and order up a cocktail from the waitress.

Lot 61

550 W. 21st St. (btw. 10th and 11th Aves.) Chelsea 212-243-6555

So, you want to feel pretty? Dress yourself up in your newest strappy sandals and head to Lot 61 where the men are hot, but the clothes are hotter. Because of its locale, fashionisti and models call Lot 61 home, but so do lots of others, which is why the bar is always bustling. Up front, you'll be hard pressed walking through the crowd without losing half of your cosmo, but the loungey back area serves as a comfy respite.

On Getting Taxis

It's pouring. Your hair is in severe danger of frizzing. You've only got ten minutes to get to the other side of town. You need a cab. Now. This is no time to be nice. Not in this game. Given the chance, anyone would steal your taxi—no matter if you've been standing there for five minutes or five hours. So, stand your ground. Be light on your feet. Run at the first sign of a lit-up number, and know your route. You haven't the moments to waste getting scammed by that Third-Avenue-by-way-of-Sixth-Avenue nonsense. You've got places to go, people to see. So remember these rules to keep your cool:

- **Don't start muttering** words of disgust to yourself. This only makes you look crazy—and therefore, an unattractive customer.

- **Do make friends** with competing taxi-hailers. If you can tell them your sob story, they will be less likely to push you away from the door when the time comes. Feel free to embellish wherever necessary.

- **Don't keep walking** about. The order of the universe clearly dictates that once you've left the corner you've been waiting at, a taxi will show up at that very spot for the next person in line.

- **Don't forgo** a taxi because it is headed in the wrong direction. This is no time to be tightfisted.

- **Do ask your taxi** driver how they are doing. Make friendly jokes to lighten things up a bit. Let him know that your lateness is in no way his fault. Take heart against those passengers that blame their tardiness on the innocent drivers. Let him/her know that you are horrified by that sort of behavior. Your new buddy will be much more apt to rush you to your destination.

- **Rushing can often** lead to forgetfulness, so always ask for a receipt, so that you can track down the taxi in the event you've left something behind.

Lotus

409 W. 14th St. (btw. 9th and 10th Aves.) West Village 212-243-4420

With Moomba dead and buried (or off to L.A., whichever way you want to look at it), Lotus is the club synonymous with swank in the big city. If swank is what you want, than swank is what you're gonna get via ambiance, well-heeled clientele, and a multitude of martini glasses. Get the most mileage as possible out of the jaunt by calling up anyone you know to say, "I'm going to Lotus tonight," or "I think I'll head over to Lotus this evening." Pass the bouncers (if you can) by being on a list or feigning that you should be (and of course dressing the part with as many Madison Avenue labels as you can manage), and head to the basement or second level where the likes of Frederika boogie down. Otherwise you can make a dinner reservation and indulge in some haute cuisine and do the whole movie star bit. DJs know exactly which songs will get the crowd to their teetering boots, from R&B to popular house. There's plenty of seating for those with two left feet (or those who thought their heels would not create excruciating pain before 4am). Expect a heavy price for cocktails, and a $25 cover. But, just think, you'll be able to start sentences with, "When I went to Lotus..."

Man Ray

147 West 15th St. (btw. 5th and 6th Aves.) Chelsea 212-929-5000

In the spirit of Chinese restaurants of yore, this scenester spot plays up the Asian motif with gilt detail, majestic high-backed seating, bamboo galore and open cooking stations. Man Ray has been much-hyped and long-awaited, and maybe that's the reason it is a bit disappointing, no matter how many Chloe-clad, hipster-belted beauties walk through the door (men in these places are frequently let-downs). Sponge painted walls and faux stained glass seemed to cheapen the whole package, but the service is great, and the spot gets packed. Downstairs, you'll find a darker, more intimate dining room, rich with reds and candlelight. Try the sopapillas — sweet fried dough — it's one of the house specialties.

The Park

118 10th Ave. (at 17th St.) Chelsea 212-352-3313

This bar makes the top-five list hands down. For starters, take a look at the thirty-foot dracaena tree in the main dining room, then there's the comfortable feeling that overtakes you upon entering the hunting-lodge-inspired lounge (like you've just come in from a snow storm). In spring and summer, the enormous garden opens up to create a breathtakingly lush space, with lots of seating. Your best bet is to save up some extra cash and make a dinner reservation, because the food, with rustic French and Italian influences, is all the buzz, and most of all, because even the bouncers admit you'll wait for at least a half an hour to get in on a weekend without one. The front bar area has a bit of a Bowery Bar feel (no wonder, since the proprietor duo created that landmark bar as well) with a 50's flavor à la glossy bricks in primary colors and a faux fireplace. Take a trip through the dining room, or the brick-lined side passage to the back Asian lounge, where scenesters sip expensive cocktails and try to scam their way into the VIP lounge. After midnight the space gets jammed, but there is an unbelievable energy that so many spots seem to lack.

Pastis

9-11 Little W. 12th (at 9th Ave.) West Village 212-929-4844

It truly is amazing what a mention in Vogue's fashion-week report will do for a new restaurant. Since its opening, Pastis has remained the It restaurant for celebs and fashionisti who have a taste for all things French. Sister to Balthazar, another McNally success, Pastis will fully satisfy your craving for fabulousness.

Sugar

311 Church St. (btw. White and Lispenard Sts.) TriBeCa

212-431-8642

Now's the time to thank God you are a woman (as opposed to those other times when you're having your period or worrying about not having your period). According to co-owner Joey Luera, women have an easier time passing the bouncer than men, who "get drunk and start fights." Having breasts is only the first requirement, though. Your best bet is to call ahead and ask for "clearance." They'll determine if you fit the desired demographic--"mature, responsible people who dress nice and fit into the savvy New York mold"—by asking questions, like what job title you hold. "If I think you're right, I'll put your name on the list; if not, I'll have to say 'sorry, I can't help you.' " Otherwise, you can let the hand of fate, or rather, Sugar's gatekeeper visually appraise you upon arrival. On the night I went, after giving my name and passing on my card, I was still made to feel like a mad cow getting herded up for slaughter. Once inside, I found a Brady Bunch-inspired interior, which was pleasing to the eye, and a mega-crowd of terribly tipsy men and women who thought nothing of reaching over you to command cocktails and taking forever in the loo. Not to fret though, as the cycle of NYC bars goes, by the time this book has reached you, Sugar will most probably have either quieted down to a tolerable space or changed hands.

Suite 16

127 8th Ave. (at 16th St.) Chelsea 212-627-1680

Who would have thought that Re-Bar, once swarming with B&Ts dancing to "Murder She Wrote," would be transformed into a swanky scene? Now a regular stop on the après-soirée celeb route, Suite 16 can be a rough place to get into late night (especially on Thursdays for Noah Tepperberg and Jason Strauss's party). Inside, the sleek leather-aluminum décor meets all haute requirements, as does the trendy drink menu. If you want guaranteed admittance, management suggests reserving a table for 6 to 15 persons; you'll have to pay a two-bottle minimum. *Karaoke Mondays (see page 115). Cover charge from $5-$20.*

TanDa

331 Park Ave. S. (btw. 24th and 25th Sts.) Gramercy 212-253-8400

When someplace new comes along from anyone associated with Moomba, there's bound to be some buzz about it. The second floor bar at this Southeast Asian eatery claims to be setting a new trend in the chichi scene—no attitude. Let's hope this velvet-rope ban catches on. The chef, Stanley Wong debuts on the New York restaurant scene, serving up signature dishes like Balinese roasted duck. Save room for dessert courtesy of pastry chef Wendy Israel.

Tao

42 E. 58th St. (Madison and Park Aves.) Midtown 212-888-2288

Tao is not for the minimal-minded. From the giant Buddha that watches over the space, to the immense space itself, low-lit with equally large-scale bamboo lanterns, and even the star-studded galas thrown at this midtown Asian restaurant—this place is over-the-top through and through. Amidst such glitz and contrivance, you'll wonder just exactly where they've hidden the slot machines and roulette table. The crowd is always large and mixed—part LA, part Upper East Side, part In-Style reader, part older men trying to pick up intoxicated young women.

Thom's Bar

60 Thompson St. (btw. Spring and Broome Sts.) SoHo 212-431-0400

Looking for the perfect seduction scene? Thom's Bar, on the second floor of 60 Thompson (an elegant boutique hotel) has all the subtle luxe (rich fabrics, contemporary sleek lines and intimate seating arrangements) you could ever need to sweep him off his feet. And apparently, I'm not the only one who thinks so. The space is couple-dominated, with so much cuddling and nuzzling one could actually die of jealousy, if one were affected by that sort of thing. When the weather's right, a back area with retractable roof nearly doubles the space. In that clandestine spirit that characterizes the new chic, 60 Thompson could easily be mistaken for an apartment building, since the hotel's check-in area is not at ground level (walking back and forth down the street ten times can definitely ruin the mood).

Green with Envy

High society. Page Six. Fashion Fiction. At first when I read about Bungalow 8 back in Plum Sykes's *Vogue* column, I was drawn in, even found myself keying in the Beverly Hills Hotel name derivative to conduct a fruitless Internet search, but then realized, alas, that the business with the key card entrance for select members must have been part of the hysterical exaggeration that make Pepper and Taylor's electronic correspondence so entertaining. How naïve you are, I thought. The bit about the helicopters and overnight packs with bikinis and bathrobes for last minute Hamptons jaunts, ordering food from any place you'd like, the cordless phones at each table—upon further consideration all seemed like wonderful products of an active imagination. New York nightlife hasn't really gotten that ridiculous. But after a few months went by, I began to hear more about this VIP club for Lot 61 devotees. *Times*, *W, New York Magazine*. Private parties for glossy-haired socialites carrying mini-champagne bottles with straws. The media manages to enchant me once again. While half of my brain rationalized, "God, that is so over the top," the other half cried, "I have to go!"

So when I was granted entrée, I carefully considered who was Bungalow 8-worthy. A guy (I selfishly decided) was a bad choice, as he would interfere in the fantasy I'd cooked up of meeting a delicious celebrity boy who would immediately fall for my refreshing down-to-earth personality. But who, oh who, was I to take? I finally settled on one of my closest friends, who felt rather nervous at the prospect of mixing with the society set. I could relate. We both decided that stressing over what to wear was a fruitless cause, since there would be no chance of purchasing a Fendi bag, a perfectly-hanging hipster belt and $300 deconstructed vintage tee-shirt in the next 48 hours just to keep up with the Joneses.

All this really meant was that we put off worrying about what to wear to keep up with the Joneses, Hiltons, J-Lo's and otherwise beautiful, wonderful, make-you-pull-in-your-stomach-and-regret-eating-that-bagel types, until the day of, at which point our reasonable thinking all of a sudden appeared much less reasonable. As a matter of fact, it actually appeared downright unreasonable. How could we go to The Hottest, Hippest call-in-your-favors, sell-your-soul-to-the-society circle, new out-Lotusing-Lotus bar without the hottest-hippest-call-in-your-favors clothing?

"I'm not having it," I told Ally on the phone at 2:54pm that Friday.

"What? I can't hear you, I have a shirt stuck over my ears," she screamed into the phone. After she successfully rescued herself from the binding Laundry tank she had paid for on her overdraft (with hopes of returning the next day), we admitted that we had both erred when deciding to come as we are.

"I went to Bloomie's, H&M, 8th Street and all of SoHo," she admitted. "Nothing."

"No way! You totally suck—I can't believe you didn't take me along!"

"Well, you were so downright set on making a statement on, how was it you put it? Oh yeah, 'the materialistic gentrification of society that has turned even the most trivial event into a contest, stripping all Americans of their morals.' So, I was actually afraid to tell you that I had given in. I thought you might take someone else."

"Did you actually believe all of that? That was my hangover talking. That was my crazy, lunatic, evil twin talking—the evil twin who has now left me at 3:00 with ABSOF***INGLUTELY nothing to wear to Bungalow 8! Now get your ass over to Saks and meet me on the 4th Floor. Girl, we've got shopping to do."

One and a half hours and two pissed off salesgirls later, we were pondering a Marc by Marc Jacobs wrap shirt and wondering if we could find a tailor to hem a $150 pair of Jill Stuart jeans in twenty minutes. Sitting on the floor near the register, we were looking over our spoils with heads in hands.

"None of this feels right," said Ally.

"Um, ladies, you're going to have to get up. There's no sitting on the floor here."

That sealed the deal. We weren't making any purchases there. The shirt didn't match with any of my shoes. The jeans Ally wanted required a specific belt, which was nowhere to be found. All seemed hopeless. And there was still hair to do! Nails to be painted! Makeup to be applied; last minute situps to attend to.

Outside Saks, we decided to rummage H&M—you never know—and then out of desperation, we ran the seemingly thousands of blocks to the Gap (of all places), weeped over the windows at Gucci, Burberry, Calvin Klein and Donna Karan, and then even the vendors selling Pashminas (why can't they be in style now that they're cheap?) seemed to require a quick look "just in case."

I was banging on the door at Roberto Cavalli when Ally smacked me across the face. "Get a hold of yourself! You've totally lost it. What the hell are you going to afford in there?" she asked.

She was right. This was a fruitless search. And then it came to me, like a ray of sunshine from the clouds. I had to call Patricia! Patricia Sellestan—the PR maven I'd interviewed the week before for an article on how five women prepare for a date. She had shown me her closet. She had walked me through the scores of Gucci samples the design house sent her season after season. She had allowed me to pour over the 400 pairs of stilettos in her collection. She had permitted me to try on the Joseph slacks. She was...my size! She had to help me. She had to let me borrow something. So, we took the subway back to my apartment, pressed the elevator incessantly, hoping to speed up its snail-like descent to the lobby, and when the door slid open at the arrival of my floor we ran frantically to my apartment. We waded through the knee-deep clothing littering the floor and found her telephone number on my computer. We crossed our fingers.

Riiiiiing. Riiiiing. "Hi. You've reached Patricia Sellestan's line. She's either away from her desk or on the other line. If this is an emergency, you can call her mobile at 917-***-****. Otherwise leave a message and she will return your call as soon as possible. Thank you and have a nice day."

This qualified as an emergency, right? A downright Sartorial 911 call was in order and I was stepping up to the plate.

Exactly one hour later Patricia Sellestan was my new best friend, and Ally had already promised she could be her maid of honor—should she ever get married. I was clad in one pair of rhinestone Jimmy Choos, Juicy Jeans and one extremely perfect Chloe top, crafted with the perfect amount of ruffles, and asymmetrical free-floating panels, paired with one Ursule Beaugeste low-slung leather belt, offsetting the sultry look with a bit of hard-edged flair. Ally settled on a black Gucci mini, thigh-high black Manolo boots and a simple lingerie-inspired tank. It was like a dream.

And then, seven hours later, after a mani/pedi (the perfect Esse shade of Ballet Slippers) a top-notch blowout (favor from frequently written about hairstylist) and makeup application (favor from frequently written about makeup artist), an excruciating abs session, a few sets of arm exercises, a few wasted minutes (okay, exactly 22) spent in front of the mirror examining the effects of my "workout," after dressing, and calling everyone I know to tell them what I was wearing (taking the once-in-a-lifetime chance of saying, "Yes, C-H-L-O-E,"), it all culminated into the creation of (if I do say so myself) one fabulous-like me.

But, what happened next was (in my mind) equal to the pre-resolution stage of Cinderella, Pretty Woman, Legally Blonde and Bridget Jones's Diary all stacked up together. My dream, it appeared, had turned into a nightmare.

At first, all was going smoothly. We were drinking $15 mojitos beneath the façade of the pink Cadillacs, glimmering swimming pools and bubble-gum-hued bungalows, watching as the A-listers smooched, drank, smoked and tried not to look like they were comparing waist and breast sizes. Paging through the menu of services, we wondered just how many people would order the use of a cordless phone in the age of cells (but still thought how extremely cool it was to have the option), how many persons are in need of a personal shopper in the middle of the night, and why it would be so difficult to run home and grab a bikini and bathrobe of your own if you decide to head out to the Hamptons before the sun comes up. But, we did employ our most diligent self-control on withholding from the purchase of that iconic cherry printed Shoshanna halter bikini.

We were, in short, having expensive, well-dressed, "but is my hair frizzing?" and "is there lipstick on my teeth?" fun, well, of sorts. We had fun thinking about whom we would telephone to say we saw so-and-so, and what's-his-name, and to ask "guess who Mr. X is dating?" We wondered by cocktail number three—would our credit cards be declined? But, decided to worry about that later. It's amazing how simple it is to put off a little worry like that when you've drunk one clear limey drink, one pink sugary one and one tart green one.

So, all was going relatively well until the alcohol began to give me a bit of confidence—or rather, over-confidence. So when I saw a super-hot so-and-so, rumored to be newly separated from his hi-profile girlfriend, I thought it a perfect time to walk the path to the loo, that as luck would have it, required me to pass right by him. So, I shared my plan with Ally. She was a rock of support. I grabbed my green apple martini and began my jaunt. Slowly, confidently, sultry-like, I swept my hair behind my ear and gave him a look right in the eye. And what a look I got in return! But, without my eyes available to navigate my route, my route navigated me—right into the back of one fiery-haired television wardrobe guru—and right onto the floor, green apple martini contents transferring too-quickly to stop from glass to C-H-L-O-E top. I'd love to tell you that super-hot-so-and-so came to my rescue, ordered me up an emergency outfit from the house concierge and whisked me off to the Hamptons to forget about everything, declaring his love for me and sweetly suggesting names for our future three children (Baskin, Toby and Paige). But none such thing happened. As I opened my eyes to reveal the scores of glitterati with hands over gaping mouths, I noticed that one of those cupped hands was clasped onto the face of a towheaded model-type whose other hand was clasped onto the shoulder of none other than super-hot so-and-so. That's when Ally came to my rescue, dragged me from the scene and called a cab for us to head back to the Reservoir, where stain and all, I knew I belonged.

When finally, I lay my dizzy head to rest that evening (or morning, rather), with visions of imminent dry-cleaning debacles, elaborate excuses and skirting phone calls from the woman I feared I would most likely have shared the most short-lived best friendship in history with, it occurred to me that perhaps the fabulous life should, in fact, be reserved for...the fabulous.

All that partying can sure make a girl hungry. Whether late-night is your prime munching time, or you're more of a morning-after eater, you've got choices aplenty at these spots.

Perhaps your carb-free diet has got you dreaming of nothing but bagels, or maybe you just need a break from The Zone. After a night on the town, you're a woman on a mission, and that mission is to eat exactly what you want. If you're going to cheat, well, by gumbo, you'd better do it right. At 4am it's so much easier to bend the rules. And yes, it's so much more fun, too. Pizza, French food, Chinese, Korean BBQ, Moroccan, or even a garlic pickle—they're all great—especially late.

Around the Clock 24 Hour

8 Stuyvesant St. (at 3rd Ave.) East Village 212-598-0402

As the name suggests, this joint is open 24 hours. And what that means is that the staff you'll find at 4am is working all night. And what that means is that the service isn't great. A few selections from the menu, however, are. Try the fruit crepes ($5.95), the carrot ginger dressing on a salad ($3.25), or any type of omelette (starting at $4.25). Note: Stuyvesant St. forks off from E. 9th St.

Big Nick's Burger Joint

2175 Broadway (between 76th and 77th Sts.) Upper West Side 212-362-9238

Choose from about 30 different burger options ($4-$6). But, if you just have to be different (and want to ignore the name) there are alternatives: pizza, steaks, fries, and omelettes are available. *Appetizers: $4-$8, entrees: $4-$15. Open 24 hours.*

Café Noir

32 Grand Street (at Thompson St.) West Village 212-431-7910

Mediterranean goodies go great with a pitcher of sangria, in case you were wondering. You'll have to do the fries thing—and forget about requesting Weight Watchers portions. *Appetizers: $3.75-$23, entrees: $6-$23.50. Open till 4 am.*

Cafeteria

119 7th Ave. (at 17th St.) Chelsea 212-414-1717

Stop in for chicken and waffles (yes, that's chicken and waffles), salads, daily specials or starters like fried calamari, all served in industrial-chic environs. *Appetizers: $5-$9, entrees: $7.50-$17.50. Open Mon.-Sun. 24 hours.*

Corner Bistro

331 W. 4th St. (at Jane St.) West Village 212-242-9502

The burgers at this rustic little pub are perennially voted among the best in town. Also on the menu: chicken sandwiches, BLTs, fries, chili and grilled cheese. *All dishes à la carte: $2.75-$5.75. Orders taken until 3:30am.*

Delta Grill

700 9th Ave. (at 48th St.) Hell's Kitchen 212-956-0934

If you happen to be going out in the Times Square area, you're in for a hectic evening. But, at least you can eat fattening Cajun food to ease the pain induced by the noise and crowds. What better thing for ladies to eat than fried green tomatoes? Also try: crawfish popcorn, shrimp creole, and jambalaya. *Appetizers: $6-$11, entrees: $9-$22. Open till 4am.*

Empire Diner

210 10th Ave. (at 22nd St.) Chelsea 212-243-2736

A longtime post-club stop for classic diner favorites. Don't worry, you'll go to the gym tomorrow. Sure you will. *Appetizers: $3.50-$18.95, entrees: $4.75-$18.50. Open 24 hours (except Tues. 4am-8:30am).*

Florent

69 Gansevoort St. (btw. Greenwich and Washington Sts.)
West Village 212-989-5779

Whether you opt for moules frites, or midnight breakfast, this West Village retro diner with a gourmet menu serves up big, yummy portions to the fashion set—and the dessert should not be skipped. *Open Fri.-Sat. 24 hours, Sun.-Thurs. 9am-5am. Appetizers: $4.50-$9.50, entrees: $6-$18.50.*

French Roast Café

78 W. 11th St. (at 6th Ave.) West Village 212-533-2233

2340 Broadway (at 85th St.) Upper West Side 212-799-1533

These sister establishments offer all things French, like jumbo-sized coffee drinks, sandwiches, salads, frites and traditional breakfast fare on their overnight menu. While service is notoriously slow, and the food is by no means outstanding, French Roast is what it is: French food that you can eat in the middle of the night. *Appetizers: $5-$9, entrees: $8-$15. Open 24 hours.*

Giant Bagel Shop

120 University Pl. (at 13th St.) West Village 212-243-2775

Although Jennifer Aniston has sworn off carbs (there have been rumors of once-per-month scoopings and fat-free cream cheese smears), the lot of us females crave them late night. All you need is a dollar or so for one of these holed pieces of heaven (or devil's food, depending on the day), so big, you can really enjoy the experience for as long as humanly possible. Smears of flavored tofu, and fat-free cream cheeses are available to top off your bagel (about $1.75). *Open 24 hours.*

Gray's Papaya

2090 Broadway (at 72nd St.) Upper West Side 212-799-0243

402 6th Ave. (at 8th St.) West Village 212-260-3532

If a date brings you here, run screaming in the other direction, but if you feel like chowing on greasy hotdogs, stop in for the $1.95 special—that's two dogs and a frozen drink that will most definitely hit the spot. *Open 24 hours.*

Kang Suh

1250 Broadway (at 32nd St.) Midtown West 212-564-6845

Got a hankering for DIY Korean BBQ in the middle of the night? Choose from meat, pork, chicken or fish. Side dishes, rice, soups, noodle dishes, sushi and sashimi also available. *Appetizers: $7-$8, entrees: about $22. Open 24 hours.*

L'Express

249 Park Ave. S. (at 20th St.) Flatiron 212-254-5868

Who couldn't go for Eggs Benedict at 3:30 am? French food in a bustling café, with friendly, if not efficient, service is what L'Express is all about. Sit, chat, make bets on how long it will take to get your check — have another coffee, you know you need it. *Appetizers: $5-12, entrees: $7-$19. Open 24 hours.*

Olive Tree Café

117 MacDougal St. (btw. W. 3rd and Bleecker Sts.) West Village 212-254-3480

If someone hadn't taken you here before, you could easily walk right by Olive Tree without noticing it. But, then you would miss out on a massive menu of treats like hearty burgers and fries, and Middle Eastern dishes. Try the hot Russian borscht — it's a family recipe ($7.50). If you're still "thirsty," mixed drinks are cheap here—$3.75-$4.25. It's all brick and coziness inside, and Crayolas are provided for paper-tablecloth drawing. Chess and backgammon available for $1 an hour. *Appetizers: about $4.50, entrees: $4.25-$8.75. Open Mon.-Thurs. 11am-4am, Fri.-Sat. 11am-5am.*

P.J. Clarke's

915 3rd Ave. (at 55th St.) Midtown East 212-759-1650

If you're seated before 3:45am, you can feast on American classics like burgers, salads, porterhouse steaks, and salmon at this NYC landmark, which has been around in some incarnation or another since the 1920's. *Appetizers: $4.10-$5.60, entrees: $8-$16. Open till 4am.*

Sarge's

548 Third Ave. (between 36th and 37th Sts.)
Murray Hill 212-679-0442

After a night of drinking, what warms a woman's heart better than an array of pickles and coleslaw at a female-owned NY deli? Pair the dills and slaw with some matzoh balls, a mile-high turkey sandwich and a Dr. Brown's black cherry soda and you'll forget all about that guy who asked your name six times and then "forgot" to ask for your phone number. *Appetizers: $4.95-$8.95, entrees: $12.95-$22.95. Open 24 hours.*

7A

109 Ave. A (at 7th St.) East Village 212-673-6583

Salads, burgers and all that jazz. Great food, all the time. Which is why party-goers often end their evenings here. *Appetizers: $3.95-$6.95, entrees: $6.50-$13.95. Open 24 hours.*

St. Mark's Pizza

3rd Ave. (btw. St. Mark's Place and 9th St.)
East Village 212-387-8037

The aroma of St. Marks Pizza gives that emanating from McDonald's (two doors down) a run for its money. This is big, cheesy pizza with toppings galore. Plain slice: $1.95. *For toppings you'll pay between $2.75- $3.50. Open Sun.-Wed. till 2am. Thurs.-Sat. till 5:30am.*

Stingy Lulu's

129 St. Mark's Pl. (between 1st St. and Ave. A)
East Village 212-674-3545

Stingy Lulu's is more than kitsch and drag queens. The staff is friendly and the food is great for the price — Caesar salads, pastas, sandwiches — it's all here. *Appetizers: $4-$6, entrees: $8-$12. Open Sun.-Thurs. till 4am, Fri.-Sat. till 5am.*

Veselka

144 2nd Ave. (at 9th St.) East Village 212-228-9682

Ultra-heavy Polish food, like potato pierogies, tastes great late. Less ethnic, but equally greasy and fattening breakfast and dinner foods also available. This is hardly the Ritz, but for less than $10, you'll be full and probably regretting every morsel that passed your lips. *Open 24 hours.*

Wo Hop

17 Mott St. (downstairs) (below Canal St.) Chinatown 212-267-2536

While there are two restaurants stacked on top of each other at this address, late night diners (DJs, bouncers, club-kids and chain-smoking local teens) in the know head straight downstairs. Try the shrimp with black bean sauce and splurge on the fried rice. *Appetizers: $5-$10, entrees: $5-$10. Open 24 hours.*

Yaffa Café

97 St. Mark's Pl. (between 1st Ave. and Ave. A)
East Village 212-674-9302

Not widely recognized for stellar service, Yaffa is known for cheap food that tastes good and fills you up. Namely — fresh salads with carrot-ginger dressing, chicken curry or stir-fry, and of course diner-like mainstays such as breakfast food (served midnight-4am weekdays; midnight-10:30am weekends) and burgers. The back garden — big and peaceful (if in fact a waitstaff wasteland) stops seating at 10:15pm. *Appetizers: $3.50-$5.95, entrees: $4-$13. Open 24 hours.*

BRUNCH

Morning-after blahs? Do the Brunch Thing. With friends, or even without, sitting at a café table munching on comforting eats like Eggs Benedict, or even a greasy omelet or a dollop of caviar can make the world seem brighter.

Pricing Guide (including drinks): $: 10-20; $$: 20-30; $$$: 30 and up.

Coffee Shop

29 Union Sq. W. (at 16th St.) Flatiron 212-243-7969

Brunch served: Sat. and Sun. 8am-4pm

No reservations **$**

Best to have the most patient friend in the group stop over early to wait for a table, because when the weather's nice the queue is absolutely not. And although the service is slower than the N train on a weekend, the food hits the spot and there's just something about sitting across from Union Square Park that does a hangover good.

Blue Ribbon Bakery & Cafe

33 Downing St. (at Bedford St.) West Village 212-337-0404

Brunch served: Sat and Sun. 11:30am-4pm

Reservations only taken for parties of 5 or more **$$**

Believe me I know, when you wake up after a long night out, sometimes you just don't want breakfast food. At Blue Ribbon Bakery & Café (don't confuse this outpost with the sister locations, which do not serve brunch) you can order anything you want à la carte from the full menu or the brunch menu — both a mix of classic French and modern American cuisine. French Toast, poached eggs with a mix of goodies like shrimp and bacon hash, smoked salmon, cheese plates, fresh fish, sandwiches — it's all available to feast on in a delightful farmhouse kitchen setting.

Petrossian

182 W. 58th St. (at 7th Ave.) Midtown West 212-245-2214

Brunch served: Sat. and Sun. 11:30am - 3pm

Reservations suggested for Sundays and holidays **$$$**

C'mon, you know you want to. Indulge. Spoil yourself rotten with goodies like caviar, foie gras and smoked salmon from the à la carte menu, or opt for a more traditional breakfast from the three-course prix fixe menu ($28—all items also available à la carte). Inform guys to dress one step above shorts, sneakers and a baseball cap.

The Vinegar Factory Café

429 E. 91st St. (btw. York and 1st Aves.) Upper East Side

212-987-0885

Brunch served: Sat. and Sun. 8am-4:30pm

No reservations taken. **$$$**

One-flight up from Eli Zabar's gourmet grocery, The Vinegar Factory is open only for weekend brunch. Serious foodies gather here to choose from delights that include a salad bar stocked with luscious Zabar's items. Notoriously expensive traditional à la carte brunch treats include egg dishes, cheese plates, French toast, caviar, salmon and plenty of desserts of the irresistible variety.

Beauty Guide *

Whether you're high-maintenance, or like to keep things simple in the beauty department, there's no denying the boost that comes with looking and feeling great. Perhaps you'd like someone else to style your locks for the evening (who wouldn't?) or maybe you'd like to try a new shade of lipstick, since you've been wearing the same one for three years (you know who you are), or maybe, just maybe, you love the way a new coat of polish looks on your digits. On the more personal side—maybe you've got a "serious" date (depending on who you are, that could be number one, or five or twenty-five, or the day you're thinking you might be getting the question popped, or even walking down the aisle), which would require some more specialized attention—maybe you were born with a bit more hair than you'd like on your face/your arms/under your chin. Read on for your beauty "yellow pages"—a resource guide to all sorts of primping, pampering and pruning, as well as a list of stores that stock all the DIY and at-home accoutrements you could ever want…or need.

FACIALS

"Facials should be scheduled every two to three months, depending on your skin's condition," says Acqua Beauty Bar's Jamie Ahn, "But in summer, you may need to go a bit more frequently; all of that time spent out in the hot weather, and even air conditioning can lead to excessively clogged pores and breakouts." Today's extensive spa menus offer myriad facials—from "oxygen" to "glycolic"—to cleanse and refresh all skin types. Refrain from scheduling a facial just before going out. Allow at least a week before a big event, since extractions (manual removal of dirt and sebum from pores) can cause redness, and blemishes may appear as a result of oil that has been brought to the surface.

Acqua Beauty Bar

7 E. 14th St. (btw. 5th Ave. and University Pl.), Flatiron 212-620-4329

With a menu that marries traditional Asian techniques with modern technology and old-fashioned indulgence, this pristine spa, adorned with rice-paper lanterns and touches of bamboo, is a 14th-Street Shangri-la. Facials are customized to address both physical and wellness needs, mixing products from Yon Ka Paris, Wu, and a house-brewed herbal line, with aromatherapy, reiki, ear reflexology and cold stones. Acqua is the first spa in New York to perform facials utilizing the L.A.-based Sonya Dakar line (you can also purchase the products to take home). Choose from their full menu of massages and body treatments. *Open Mon. and Thurs. 10am-9pm, Tue., Wed., Fri. 10am-8pm, Sat.-Sun. 10am-7pm. Facials start at $85.*

Bliss 57

19 E. 57th St. (btw. Madison and 5th Aves.) Midtown East

212-219-8970

Have a busy lifestyle that won't allow for all-day pampering, but don't want to skimp on the luxe? Bliss 57 understands and therefore offers simultaneous services like facial treatments (try the oxygen blast for a quick pre-party pick-me-up, $80), manicure ($22) and pedicure ($45). And while you're waiting for your nails to dry in the "blissful" ocean-inspired lounge, take a seat on the soft suede banquette, skim through a magazine, and enjoy some lemonade, soda or a glass of wine, and decadent munchies. Everything here is smooth sailing, from check-in (when you receive a

Cosmetics for Cocktails

Makeup artist Jenni Lee on lifting your after-dark looks with makeup:

Spot Treatment

With a tiny brush, dot cream foundation (rather than concealer) over blemishes. With fingertips, apply foundation to the whole face, then top it with a powder. Again dot a bit more foundation right on the pimples and repeat the re-application until coverage is complete.

Sneaky Cheek Bones

Perhaps your cheekbones are your strongest feature; perhaps you can't say you've ever seen yours before. Either way, you can enhance them by sweeping a foundation-brush dabbed with skin-toned highlighter from the corners of the mouth to ears and along the jawline. Then retrace the whole process, this time brushing peach (for fair to medium skin tones), or pink blush (for darker skin tones) and finish off with a bit more color underneath the jaw line and at the base of your neck.

Perfect Pout

Line lips, then use the same pencil to fill in, otherwise you'll end up with a ring around your mouth when lipstick rubs off. Apply a shimmery gloss over lip pencil in white, pale pink or peach.

mesh bag packed with a waffle robe, Sensa slippers and Bliss bottled water), to the changing room (just take the key from any available locker), to the services (professional and indulgent all the way), to your pre-exit primp (showers, soap, shampoo, conditioner, contact lens solution, cellophane-wrapped brushes and combs, mouthwash and deodorant are yours for the using). *Mon.-Tue., Thu.,-Fri. 9:30am-8:30pm, Wed. 12:30pm-8:30pm, Sat. 9:30am-6:30pm, Sun. closed. 30 min facial $60, 30 min massage $60. Book several months in advance. Insider tip: call the evening before the day you'd like to go and snag a last minute cancellation.*

Glow Skin Spa

41 E. 57th St. (btw. Madison and Park Aves.) Midtown East

212-319-6654

When you've got to look perky all over, schedule a facial and breast firming treatment at Glow. What, you never thought of toning your ta-tas? I highly recommend it. And the proprietor duo at this friendly little spa knows your time is precious, so you can have them tag-team you with the two services: that's total upper-body beauty in 60 minutes. Also check out their stress-reduction facials and ask about a simultaneous foot reflexology for head-to-toe treatments. Products by Essensa, NV Perricone, Peter Thomas Roth and more. *By appointment only. Breast firming treatment $45, facials start at $95, waxing: brows $30, bikini starts at $30. First time clients receive 10% off of services.*

Paul Labrecque Salon & Spa
at The Reebok Sports Club

160 Columbus Ave. (at 57th St.) Midtown East

212/595-0099 or 1-888-PLSALON

Facials here (six varieties, including *bacials* for the back, oxygen facials and aromatherapy facials) are performed with a top-of-the-line product base in a no-rush environment and priced from $100-160 (with package discounts). Spa clients can also make use of the Reebok Sports Club's Jacuzzi, wet steam and dry sauna rooms. Full spa and hair salon menus are available. Retail shelves are chockablock with all the best goodies like YonKa Paris, Shu Uemura, and Biologique Recherche. When their new outpost opens in the swanky Chatham residence (181 E. 65th St., btw. 3rd and Lexington Aves., 212/595-0099), you can bring your man along to enjoy everything from a shoeshine to a sports manicure. Both locations offer full coifing services (see hair stylists, below). *Columbus Ave. location open Mon.-Fri. 8am-11pm, Sat. 9am-8pm, Sun. 10am-8pm. Chatham location open Dec.; hours will be Mon.-Fri. 8am-10pm, Sat. 9am-8pm, Sun. 10am-7pm.*

Quick-change Face

How to switch gears from nine-to-five beauty to evening ingenue in 10 minutes or less.

That last minute memo. That ever-ringing phone. You're due to meet the ladies for a cocktail in 20 minutes. But, a look in the mirror reflects the long day you've had. Time for a bit of beauty magic. What? You don't have time to go home and re-do your whole look? No shock there. Matthew Sky's real-time do-over method will get you out of the office, and on with your life.

In the AM If, by the grace of God, you've planned ahead and already know you'll be going out after work, go light on the makeup. Skip the waterproof mascara, choose a lighter shade of lipstick. This way, removal will be a much simpler task.

Your Mini Arsenal Stock up on samples or downsized versions of lipstick, foundation, concealer, blush, mascara and shadows. Baby sizes take up less space and allow room for more products—you won't be stuck wearing one color when you're really in the mood for another. Another office must-have: a hydrating mist, like Evian's, which you can spray on throughout the day to keep yourself feeling fresh and alive.

Make a Clean Sweep Forget about adding onto, or refreshing, the makeup you've applied in the morning. Instead, invest in makeup remover towelettes (MAC makes great ones) that remove all of your makeup without having to lug soap to the ladies room. If you do have room (and time), and perhaps a private bath, Sky suggests applying some Noxema and allowing it to sit for two minutes to refresh your face.

Get Moist Smooth a moisturizer over your entire face to prevent dryness and prep skin properly.

The Best Base Skip the foundation, and dab concealer over spots and under eyes. Next, apply a light invisible powder like Christian Dior's 009 (which works on all skin colors). To top it off, brush a cream or powder blush on the apples of cheeks.

Eye Supply Mascara is a pick-me-up must. After sweeping a bit over lashes, apply shadow in the crease and sweep across the lower lids. You can even use the powder to line above the lashes in place of a pencil. Whatever you do, don't define underneath the eyes. This will only bring attention to any signs of fatigue you may already be showing.

Quick Lips Evening is the time to be more adventurous with darker lip colors. For a fuss-free finish, forget about pencils, stain lips with lipstick and then top off with a clear or complementary color gloss.

BROWS, LASHES, AND BODY HAIR

Whether you're after a quick eyebrow wax or electrolysis on your bikini line, these spots specialize in body and facial hair grooming treatments.

Allure

139 E. 55th St. (btw. 3rd and Lexington Aves.) Midtown East

212-644-5500

Waxing here is performed with painstaking attention to detail. Not one ingrown hair will be left untended (bikini $25, Brazilian $40, eyebrows $20 waxed or tweezed). Sensitive skin will benefit from the aromatherapy wax used here, made with lavender oil and vitamins. And facials ($55-$150) are also a house specialty, with about 30 customized masks made from product lines like Cellex C, Epicuren, Sothys, and exclusive to Allure—Douceur (available to take home too). Full spa and hair menu available. *Open Mon.-Fri. 10:30am-7:30pm, Sat. and Sun. 10am-6pm. Extra effort made to accommodate walk-ins and last-minute appointments.*

Butterfly

15 E. 30th St., Suite 202 (btw. 5th and Madison Aves.) Midtown East

212-685-8822

In-house brow expert Yvette Gil prefers tweezing to waxing "for its precision and minimal irritation." Schedule a brow spa treatment that starts with a consultation that actually focuses on the look you like, in addition to some expert advice—do you like them natural or more manicured? How do they grow in? Then Yvette takes a look at the shape of your eyes and face to determine the look you'll love. Next a hot cloth dipped in lavender extract and sea salt is applied across the brows to soften the skin for easier hair removal. Then comes the tweezing, trimming, application of a home-mixed gel of aloe, sea algae, chamomile extract, lavender oil and cucumber extract— a blend of healing agents to help reduce swelling and sensitivity. All of this is finished off with a cold compress—which has been soaked in cucumber water—to close the pores. Yvette fills in arches if necessary (using Laura Mercier products) and teaches you how to do it yourself. Time-permitting, she will re-touch your makeup free of charge. *Brow Spa Treatment costs $40, and takes about 20 minutes. Walk-ins accommodated if possible. Also see hair styling on page 174.*

Dyanna

40 E. 21st St. (btw. Park Ave. S. and Broadway) Flatiron

212-995-2355

Olga — a waxer, manicurist among the best of them—gets booked, so try to plan ahead. While the space may not look like much from the inside or out, models and devoted locals know quality when they see it. The full range of Esse polishes are available. A full spa menu is also offered (facials, body wraps and scrubs, epilight, massages). *Manicure: $11, pedicure $20, waxing $5-$26. Open Mon.-Fri. 10am-8pm, Sat. and Sun. 10am-6pm. Walk-ins accommodated if possible.*

Elizabeth Arden

691 Fifth Avenue at (54th St.) Midtown 212-546-0280

Although you might think of the trademark red door as a marker of your mother's generation, you may want to think again. Luxe, my ladies, is luxe. Voted as the best place for waxing by New York Magazine, EA uses a wax developed by Ms. Arden herself which is famous for not drying out skin, and gripping all of the hairs in one swoop (brows start at $23, bikini starts at $29). And getting your hair done here is just as fabulous — Elizabeth Arden offers the full gamut of hair services, along with a to-die-for product offering. 15 facial varieties ($77-$120), microdermabrasion, body treatments, massages, nails, bronzing and tons more. *Mon., Tue., Fri., Sat. 8am-6:30pm, Wed. 8am-7:30pm, Thurs. 8am-8pm, Sun. 9am-6pm. Blowouts start at $55, cuts start at $97, single process color starts at $75.*

Ella Bache

8 W. 36th St. (btw. 5th and 6th Aves.) Midtown West 212-279-8562

Founder Ella Baché was really very fond of eyelashes. So, it's no surprise (okay, it's less surprising after you hear of her affinity) that her namesake spa is home to the eyelash perm. Yes, you've read correctly. With the help of tiny rollers and some perm solution, you can have the curliest lashes in town. The treatment lasts approximately six to eight weeks. *Open Tue. 9am-5pm, Wed. 10am-8pm, Thurs. 10am-7pm, Fri. 10am-6pm, Sat. 9am-5pm. Eyelash Perm costs $50, one-hour facials start at $75.*

Eve

400 Bleecker St. (btw. W. 11th and Perry Sts.) West Village

212-807-8054

For girls on the go, Eve is a mini-treatment spa that emphasizes speed, but doesn't skimp on quality or coolness. Try their Date Wax treatment to get you ready for that special rendezvous ($50)—that's eyebrow and bikini waxing using gourmet wax, touted for its low irritation quotient—so you can literally get up and go without looking like a tomato. *Open Mon.-Fri. 11am-7pm, Sat. and Sun. 10am-6pm.*

Haven

150 Mercer St. (btw. Prince and Houston Sts.) SoHo 212-343-3515

Want to take it off, I mean—ahem—take it all off? Stop in for the Sphinx with honey wax at this SoHo spa and you'll be bare as can be ($45 standard; gourmet wax for sensitive skin $65). Haven also offers a top-to-toe assortment of treatments as well as seasonal specialties like the Sugar Fix body scrub with apple cider and brown sugar ($100), Repair facial—complete cellular repair with vitamin C (and a neat take-home kit) to help reverse free-radical damage ($85). Walk-ins accommodated when possible. *Open Mon.-Fri. 11am-7pm, Sat. 10am-6pm.*

Julie Ann Gordon

30 E. 60th St. 5th Floor (btw. Park and Madison Aves.)

Upper East Side   212-593-0239

Anyone who battles with facial hair knows that tweezing, waxing and snipping just doesn't cut it. The degree of confidence that accompanies a permanent remedy to the problem is (at the risk of sounding like an infomercial) life-changing. Stop trying to find dimly lit bars or maximum-coverage makeup. Electrolysis—although not an overnight solution—ultimately removes unwanted hair forever. Gordon is a certified electrologist with 40 years of experience, who provides scar-free, non-detectable results. She specializes in problem hairs, a.k.a. ingrowns; total body treatment available. Don't be shy—she's seen it all. By appointment only. *Open Mon.-Fri. 11am-8pm, Sat. 11am-5pm. $42 per half hour session, $75 for a full hour.*

Minardi

29 E. 61st St. 5th Floor (btw. Park and Madison Aves.)

Upper East Side 212-308-1711

Vivian Hidalgo, brow-guru, announced to me, "Your arches have collapsed." And God help me, I never realized that before. After we laughed about that for a moment, though, she got to work to show me how my brows should really look, using a relatively quick procedure, which involves tweezing, which Vivian feels, affords "less trauma to such a sensitive area". She also applied some shadow (with at-home how-to) to round out the "collapsed area." The result: sheer arch perfection. Price: about $50. Although brow treatments (color can also be done) are performed in the hair salon, Minardi has recently opened a third-floor spa, small, but relaxing and beautifully appointed. Schedule an appointment here for 11 kinds of facials ($120-$300), microdermabrasion, masks, self-tanning treatments and more. *Open for hair/eyebrows: Mon. 9am-7pm, Tue.-Thurs. 8am-9pm, Fri.-Sat. 9am-7pm. Spa open Mon.-Sat. 9am-8pm.*

Brows 101

"Eyebrows are the most important feature on the face," says makeup artist Jenni Lee. To accentuate yours, color them in with a pencil or powder shadow. Pick a shade that coordinates with the darkest shade in your hair (if your hair is dyed, match the pencil or shadow to your brow color). Using light, feathery strokes, lengthen, or fill in as needed. When shaping brows, remember the inside corner of the left brow should begin at 11 o'clock and the right at 2. Brows should arch right over the outer ends of the irises. To groom, brush brows with upward strokes with a toothbrush.

HAIR STYLING

Butterfly

(see page 170 for contact information)

This bunch of ex-John Barrett stylists brings uptown standards to a thoroughly downtown setting. If you're in need of some tress Rx, schedule a customized Kerastase conditioning treatment (the full line of take-home products also sold here). The Japanese straight perm here can even be performed on most bleached tresses. *Blowouts start at $5, cuts start at $100, single-process color starts at $100. Open Tue. 11am-7pm, Wed. 10am-6pm, Thurs. 11am-1pm, Fri. 10am-6pm, Sat. 9am-4pm.*

Damian West

152 W. 10th St. (at Waverly Pl.) West Village 212-352-2733

Specializing in color correction, Damian West is the place to take your fried, green, too-orange, too-blonde, too-dark hair for the look you really want. Also, come here for hair extensions (dyed just for you), that you can pop in, or take out whenever you'd like. *Open Tue.-Sat. 11am-7pm. Walk-ins accommodated if possible. Single process color starts at $75, partial highlights $125, blowouts start at $40, cuts start at $50.*

Federico

10 W. 55th St. (btw. 5th and 6th Aves.) Midtown West 212-262-3027

Well, there's hair color, and then there's Federico hair color. The latter is the sort that causes heads to turn, and induces questions of the genius who performed this follicular miracle. Federico's colorist, Robbie is an artiste. Try a styling session with their state-of-the-art tubular dryer that looks crazy, but works amazingly well. Most recently, Federico adds the super-duper straightening procedure we're all in awe of to his roster. *Open Mon.-Wed. 8am-7pm, Thurs 8am-8:30pm, Fri.-Sat. 8am-6pm. Cuts start at $75, single process color from $70, straightening from $600.*

Garren at Henri Bendel's

712 5th Ave, 3rd Floor (btw. 55th and 56th Sts.) Midtown 212-841-9400

Here's how popular Garren is: not only is his eponymous shop nestled in the uber-swank Bendel's, but he's styled hair for a whopping one thousand magazine covers, and there's, I'm told, a two-year waiting list to schedule a $300 cut with him. But, don't fret, there are other expert stylists at this salon who have coifed their fair share of fabulous people, and with whom you can book an appointment within two weeks time. Come here for the straightest, sleekest blowouts around. *Mon.-Wed. and Fri.-Sat. 8:45am-7pm, Thurs. 8:45am-8pm. Blowouts start at $60, cuts start at $100, single process color starts at $125.*

Glow

23rd St., 10th Floor (btw. Park and Madison Aves.) Flatiron

212-228-1822

A boutique salon with a specialty in color, Glow is trusted by women with all types of hair textures and colors in the search for the perfect hue. Check out the MOP line of organic products, on sale here. *Open Tue.-Sat. 10am-8pm. Will accommodate walk-ins if possible. Blowouts $45, cuts with blowdry $95, single process color starts at $85.*

Ouidad

846 Seventh Ave., 5th Floor (btw. 54th and 55th Sts.) Midtown West

212-333-7577

If you're serious about taming your curls, and I do mean serious, entrust those twisty tendrils to Ouidad, who's not only invented and patented a cutting technique specifically for spiraled strands, but also developed a hair-care line just for wavy manes and a "softening" procedure to relax (without damaging) ultra-tight twists. *Tue., Wed. and Fri. 9:30am -6:30pm, Thurs. 10am-7pm, Sat. 9am-5pm, summer hours for July and Aug: Mon.-Fri. 9:30am-6:30pm. Cuts run about $100, softening ranges from $140-$200, depending on hair length.*

Paul Labrecque Salon & Spa
at The Reebok Sports Club

(see page 167 for contact information)

If you're of the mind that great hair is worth a great investment, then you may want to find out if you're a good candidate for Labrecque's Thermal Reconditioning Treatment ($750), a no-nonsense straightening treatment that's got beauty editors around the country calling in favors. Imagine—wash and go hair—ahhh...*Blowouts start at $50, cuts start at $75, single process color starts at $70.*

Pierre Michel

131 E. 57th St. (at Lexington Ave.) Midtown East 212-755-9500

Seventy-five stylists, colorists, estheticians, makeup artists and manicurists are on hand at this super luxury salon, to make you look beautiful, at the standards that uptown salon-goers are accustomed to: a private color room, complimentary cappuccinos and light cuisine are all available here. *Open Mon.-Wed. and Fri.-Sat. 8:30am-6pm, Thurs. 8:30am-7pm. Blowouts start at $60, cuts start at $110, single process color starts at $85.*

Minardi

(see page 173 for contact information)

Anyone who's anyone in the beauty biz knows that a colorist who trained with Beth Minardi is the sort of master you can trust with your tresses. And the prices clearly reflect this status. This bustling uptown salon does it all. *Blowouts start at $50 ($35 after a color treatment), cuts start at $95, single process color starts at $95.*

Red

323 West 11th St. (btw. Greenwich and Washington Sts.) West Village 212-924-4667

If you're looking for the best cut in the city, look no further. This tiny, cozy three-chair salon will cut, shape, and style your strands with painstaking detail. *Open Tue.-Fri. 12pm-6:45pm (for last appt.), Sat. 11am-6pm (for last appt). Cuts start at $80, blowouts start at $45, single process color starts at $75.*

Rumor

15 E. 12th St., 2nd Floor (btw. University Pl. and 5th Ave.) West Village 212-414-0195

Sick of the heat-stroke inducing, forearm tiring, never-coming-out-like-you'd-hoped process of straightening your strands? Rumor's Hair Recovery menu boasts a Japanese Straight Perm that promises to get the kinks out (about $500), using a thermal technique with hi-tech flatirons and computer chips—which, if you can't understand, you can appreciate. Bleached blondes need not apply (sorry). If you're a curly girl who's always going the straight way, take home the Japanese home sugar-based conditioning treatment designed just for your hair from Crède Japan ($32). *Open Tue.-Fri. 10am-7pm, Sat. 9am-6pm. Walk-ins accommodated if possible. Blowouts are $45, cuts start at $80, single process color is $70.*

TRESS RX

We've all heard about the Yale study that finally puts some concrete evidence behind what we've known for years—bad hair days suck. They make you feel less confident, less fabulous. If you're going to employ common sense, you'll just realize that it's not as bad as you think, that your hair should not rule your life. But, c'mon now, when do we really employ common sense? When we head out in six-inch stilettos? When we sign over half of our salaries to pay for studio apartments that can barely house all of the things we've bought with our over-the-limit credit cards? Right. So, since we can't cope with bad hair days, we might as well learn how to abolish them. I've enlisted the help of a woman's best friend—a hairstylist—Evelyn Calderon of Butterfly Salon—to teach us how to combat mane misadventures with a bit of prevention and a dose of last-minute intervention.

Do Dilemma #1

Straightening and Flattening Frizz

Prevention Technique: Before you even think about the blow dryer, you need the right products to add moisture to your mane. The first step: a conditioning treatment—to be applied twice a week. If you're like most people, though, you hate the whole process of waiting around while the conditioner does its thing, and then re-showering to remove the stuff. For a low-fuss alternative, try Phillip B's Life Drops, which is applied before you shower (like on a lazy Saturday or while you watch *The Nanny/Friends/Frasier* before you get ready). Wash with a conditioning shampoo, like Sebastian Laminates Shampoo or L'Oreal Iridiance and then work a leave-in conditioner like Nutri-Liss from Kerastase through your hair (you can mix it with their glossifier—Serum Nutri-Instante for a more intensified effect, or for a cheaper fix, two drops of olive oil will do the trick).

HELP!!!

Last minute emergency: It's been raining/humid for days on end and you're frizz is out of control. It's time for serious intervention. A salon-strength flatiron, like the Solano, will create slick strands like nobody's business. Find them at Ray's Beauty Supply, where industry people stock up on them (212-757-0175). Tip: Do not hold the iron down on one spot; glide it through small sections from root to end—otherwise you can seriously damage your hair. Also, be advised that this type of follicular perfection is addictive; refrain from performing this ritual on a daily basis. To top it off, rake your fingers through and tug at your hairline. Give your hair a shot of cold air with a blow dryer to close the cuticle, and finish off with a glosser like Sahag Translucent Shine Spray (212-750-7772). Spray product onto palms and then work through to prevent a greasy finish.

Do Dilemma #2

Controlling Wavy or Curly Strands

Prevention Technique: Wash with gentle shampoo and apply olive oil for a bit of moisture. A great way to put the breaks on excess volume and frizz is to part hair down the middle and braid the two sections. When its dry, unbraid and gently separate strands. Otherwise, secure hair in a ponytail, twist the length of the strands around the base and secure with pins. When tresses dry, remove pins and rubber band to reveal soft, loose waves. Add a bit of pomade to create distinct sections, if desired. If you're short on time, or decide to go the more traditional route (that is–wash and style immediately), scrunch with a towel after washing, comb, gel hair, and then twist sections into spirals around your fingers to create desired coils. Whatever you do, do not scrunch while your hair is drying—this is how frizz is created! Try: Phyto #8 gel—mixed with Kerastase Nutri-Liss before styling.

Last minute emergency: Tie hair up in a clean, low ponytail, and spritz with a water bottle to refresh frizzy strands. Leave it just like that, or pin it into a chignon—neat or messy—whatever style you crave.

Do Dilemma #3

Control the Oil Spill

Prevention Technique: Oily tresses need the right shampoo. Choose one containing mint—which cleanses and controls the scalp—(look for Aveda Rosemary Mint Shampoo, or Sebastion's). Switch off with a daily shampoo if your hair gets too dry. Don't apply conditioner to the roots! Just moisturize mid-lengths to ends—with a very light product. Or skip conditioner all together and smooth a little Nutra-Liss on ends.

Last Minute Emergency: Let's say your hair's looking oily, or you've let that blow-dry go for five days. For an instant fix, spray a dry shampoo like Klorane (available at Ricky's, 212-226-5552) onto strands; it dries up the oil and makes hair look and feel clean.

Do Dilemma #4

Boost Your Boring Strands

Prevention Technique: Have your stylist cut long layers into your hair. Steer clear of heavy styling products. If you must, spritz a bit of hairspray at the ends. To style, grab sections and start twisting and scrunching to create the look you like. Allow hair to air dry and then shake it up to add extra volume. Styling aid: Bumble and Bumble South Surf Spray, which actually moisturizes your hair with kelp and algae extracts and helps create that tousled beach-hair look (800-7BUMBLE).

Last Minute Emergency: If styling time is nonexistent, and washing is not going to happen, slick hair back into a messy bun, leaving some sexy tendrils sticking out here and there.

NAILS

Acqua Beauty Bar

(see page 165)

Pedicures here are perfomed in massage chairs and utilize a whole range of prestige polishes. Super-luxe 8-step services like the Orchid pedicure (with grapefruit extract-based products) and the Burt's Bees Natural Foot Remedy (using that all-natural line's goodies) are also available. *Manicures $22, pedicures start at $40.*

BuffSpa

The Plaza Level at Bergdorf Goodman,
754 5th Ave (at 57th St.), Midtown 212-872-8624

Bergdorf Goodman's BuffSpa offers hygienic-chic manis and pedis, foot massages and eyebrow grooming on a walk-in basis. Buff's pedicure room accommodates four clients (with complementary phones). Co-owners Deborah Hardwick and John Barrett have placed a few Berdorf-worthy *objets* around the space. Manolo Blahnik sandals serve as decorative accessories, and while they're just for show (regretfully), the trendy shades of Esse polish exclusive to Buff are readily available for your twenty tips. A three-step exfoliation brings feet to party-ready standards and tea-tree salt soaks put fingers in top form. *Open Mon.-Sat. 10am-7pm (except Thurs. 10am-8), Sun. 12pm-6pm.*

Cleo Nails

270 3rd Ave. (btw. 21st and 22nd Sts.) Gramercy 212-677-4900

You rushed through that last meeting. You told your boss that you had to be home to let the air conditioner repairman in by 7pm (white lies are okay in the name of beauty). But alas, you didn't make it out of work on time. You rush to the nail place, but no amount of banging on the window and muttering under your breath will change the fact that the damned place is closed. So what do you do? Head to Cleo or sister shop Cleo 2 (just a few doors down, at 258 3rd Ave., 212-260-0300 — with prices a bit higher—$13 for manicure, $30 for pedicure), read a glossy, have a manicure ($7), a pedicure in a comfy massage chair ($21) and treat yourself to a mini shoulder massage. Now all you have to do is figure out what to wear... *Open Mon.-Sat. 9:30am-12am, Sun. 10am-11pm.*

Dyanna

(see page 171 for contact information)

The full range of Esse polishes is available for your twenty digits.

The Greenhouse

127 E. 57th St. (btw. Lexington and Park Aves.) Midtown East

212-644-4449

Say it with me — S-P-L-U-R-G-E. Indulgences are not just for women who go by single-name monikers (Madonna, Gisele). And, if you're going to do it, you might as well do it right. Voted The Best "Sybaritic Spa" by *New York Magazine*, a mani/pedi here is performed in your own private booth, stocked with television and tables for munching your gourmet lunch or reading up on the latest trends in *Vogue*. Full spa menu available. Walk-ins accommodated upon availability. *Open Mon.-Sun. 10am-7pm. Pedicures start at $50.*

Jin Soon Natural Hand and Foot Spa

56 E. 4th St. (btw. Bowery and 2nd Ave.) East Village 212-473-2047
Also at 23 Jones St. (btw. Bleecker and W. 4th Sts.) West Village

212-229-1070

The emphasis here is on nails — there are seven types of mani-pedis to choose from, like the Flower Petal Float or the Breath of Milk and Honey. Jin Soon is known citywide for her trendy, decadent pedis and "lying down manicures" in the "floating box" room. Her nail art designs range from applied jewels to hand-painted Chinese characters and camouflage patterns ($2-$7 each nail). Choose from a range of prestige polishes, from brands like Esse and Nars. Book one to two weeks in advance. Waxing services also available. *Open Mon.-Sun. 11am-8pm. Manis $15-$30, pedis $30-$60, eyebrow waxing $15-$30.*

181

SHOPPING BEAUTY

Whatever you want, whatever you need, you'll find it at one of these shops. But, don't overlook department store beauty counters (Henri Bendel, Saks Fifth Avenue, Bergdorf Goodman, Bloomingdale's, Macy's), where you can find most everything you need in one place.

Caswell-Massey

518 Lexington Ave. (at 48th St.) Midtown East 212-755-2254

"America's oldest chemists and perfumers" still provides daintily packaged fragrances, bath and body products in lots of scents like lilac, freesia and almond and aloe that make you feel pretty and feminine all over. Their New York outpost also sells Mason-Pearson hairbrushes and Aquis hair towels. *Open Mon.-Fri. 9am-7pm, Sat. 10am-6pm, Sun. 12pm-5pm.*

Demeter

83 2nd Ave. (btw. 4th and 5th Sts.) East Village 212-505-1535

Scent-sational Demeter fragrances (over 300 in all) are found at the company's only U.S. shop. And these are no ordinary scents—choose from sprays like cinnamon bun, Altoids, tomato seeds and gin tonic ($15 for 1oz, $45 for 4oz). You'll also find fragrant lotions, shower gels, oils and bath salts. *Open Mon.-Fri. 10am-6pm, Sat.-Sun 12pm-7pm.*

FACE Stockholm

224 Columbus Ave. (at 71st St.) Upper West Side 212-769-1420

110 Prince St. (at Greene St.) SoHo 212-966-9110

687 Madison Ave. (btw. 61st and 62nd Sts.) Upper East Side

212-207-8833

Hailing from Sweden, this industry favorite stocks wonderful cosmetics and tools for all skin colors. Try Trinity, a multi-purpose cream color for lips, eyes and cheeks, available in six shades ($16). *Columbus: open Mon.-Wed. 11am-7pm, Thurs.-Sat. 11am-8pm, Sun. 12pm-6pm. Prince St. open Sun.-Wed. 11am-7pm, Thurs.-Sat. 11am-8pm, Madison Ave. open Mon.-Wed. 10am-6pm, Thurs. 10am-7pm, Fri. 10am-6pm, Sat. 10am-7pm, Sun. 12pm-6pm.*

Fresh

57 Spring St. (btw. Lafayette and Mulberry Sts.) Little Italy
212-925-0099

1060 Madison Ave. (btw. 80th and 81st Sts.) Upper East Side
212-396-0344

Shop here for Fresh's cult-followed soaps from Bean Town, as well as Fresh cosmetics, body and skincare products (choose from lush lines like Soy, Milk, Sugar and Honey), and a selection of other hard-to-find brands. Spring St. *Open Mon.-Sat. 10pm-8pm, Sun. 12pm-6pm. Madison Ave. Open Mon.-Sat. 10pm-7pm, Sun. 12pm-6pm.*

Kiehl's

109 3rd Ave. (btw. 13th and 14th Sts.) East Village 212-677-3171

No-nonsense, wildly popular body, face and hair products at reasonable prices. And, God love them, generous free samples. *Open Mon.-Wed. and Fri. 10am-6:30pm, Thurs. 10am-7:30pm, Sat. 10am-6pm.*

MAC

113 Spring St. (btw. Mercer and Greene Sts.) SoHo 212-334-4641

14 Christopher St. (near 6th Ave.) West Village 212-243-4150

1 E. 22nd St. (at 5th Ave.) Flatiron 212-677-6611

Always adding new products and colors to their already extensive cosmetics line, MAC is a name that every makeup aficionado and dabbler knows well. Products also sold at Bloomingdale's, Macy's, Henri Bendel and Saks Fifth Avenue. *Spring St. open Mon.-Sat. 11am-7pm, Sun. 12pm-6pm. Christopher St. open Mon.-Sat. 12pm-7pm, Sun. 1pm-6pm. 22nd St. open Mon.-Sat. 10am-8pm, Sun. 12pm-6pm.*

Makeup Forever

409 W. Broadway (btw. Prince and Spring Sts.) SoHo
212-941-9337 or 800-757-5175

Every once in a while a cosmetics line comes along and knocks the socks off everyone. This, ladies, is one of them. Rarely a magazine photo shoot goes by without a mention, usage (or often a pilfering) of one of these desirable products. Choose from shadows, lipsticks, foundations, body paints, eyebrow and blush powder, and everything else you could need in some of the best colors around. Perfect for evening: rouge pinceau — an adorable lip color pot, complete with its own fold-away brush ($19). Prices range from $15-$40. *Open Mon.-Sat. 11am-7pm, Sun. 12pm-6pm.*

Ray's Beauty Supply

721 8th Ave. (btw. 45th and 46th Sts.) Midtown West 800-253-0993

Where the industry experts and hair-obsessed go for everything follicular. Shop here for your salon-strength flatiron and blowdryer from top names like Solano, as well as hair care lines like Aveda, Terax and Phyto. *Open Mon.-Fri. 9:30am-6pm, Sat. 10:30am-5pm.*

Sephora

635 5th Ave. (at 51st St.) Midtown 212-245-1633

130 W. 34th St. (bet. Broadway and 7th Ave.) Midtown 212-629-9135

119 5th Ave. (at 19th St.) Flatiron 212-674-3570

555 Broadway (btw. Prince and Spring Sts.) SoHo 212-625-1309

If you're going for selection, the midtown location can't be beat. It's a virtual beauty wonderland with knowledgeable sales staff in each department to guide you through the sea of products. Don't miss the fragrance floor on the lower level — breathtaking! Here you'll find all the prestige brands — from cosmetics to hair and skin care, in an environment that's more user-friendly than traditional department store counters. *51st St. open Mon.-Fri. 10am-9pm, Sat. 10am-8pm, Sun. 11am-7pm. 34th St. open Mon.-Sat. 10am-8:30pm, Sun. 11am-7pm. Fifth Ave. open Mon.-Sat. 10am-8pm, Sun. 12pm-6pm. Broadway open Mon.-Wed. 10am-8pm, Thurs.-Fri. 10am-9pm, Sat. 10am-8pm, Sun. 12pm-7pm.*

Handbags, Heels and In-Between

Looking for something fab to wear? Here's your head-to-toe shopping guide for clothing, shoes, handbags and even something sexy (or supportive, or both) underneath.

SHOES

If you're on a mission for footwear, you've got to have a plan. Head uptown to Madison Ave. (btw. 60th and 70th Sts.) for prestige, you-know-what-you're-gonna-get shoe stores like Cole-Haan, Charles Jourdan, Prada, Sergio Rossi, Bottega Veneta, Tod's and Unisa. Fifth Ave. in the 50's is similar territory: shop Salvatore Ferragamo, Prada's other outpost (also at 57th and Park Ave.), Manolo Blahnik, Jimmy Choo and Gucci. Sometimes, though, you don't have the budget to satisfy those ultra indulgences; this is when you head down to 8th St. (between 5th and 6th Aves.), familiarly referred to as "Shoe Row," where you'll find more affordable versions of all the current trends, as well as the downtown mainstays like clunky heels, Pumas, and mile-high Luichiny platforms. You'll find a few stores between 5th Ave. and Broadway, at which corner you can take a right and head downtown to find similar multi-label shops all the way to Prince St. If you still haven't found anything, you're already in SoHo, so if you're willing to up your budget, you can find lots of uptown brands and clothing designers' shoe outposts like Helmut Lang and Marc Jacobs, in addition to varied-label shoe sellers like Kerquelen, Kirna Zabête, and the downtown outpost of Otto Tootsie Plohound.

Cesare Paciotti:

833 Madison Ave (near 69th St.) Upper East Side 212-452-1222

Move over Manolo. Slip into a pair of Cesare Paciotti shoes (with sexy dagger insignia) and you'll understand why people go gaga for his footwear. If you never thought you could spend $500 on boots, see if you can live up to the challenge. It doesn't matter what you wear up top. These shoes take any outfit into high-gear. *Open Mon.-Sat. 10am-6pm.*

Bloomingdale's

1000 3rd Ave. (at 59th St.) Midtown East 212-705-2000

If you can elbow your way past the shoe-waving women trying to attract the attention of the apparently overworked salespeople, you'll have lots of brands and styles to choose from — that is, if you get there the day the stock arrives. Shoes on 2 are from labels like BCBG, Nine West and David Aaron. On the 4th floor you'll be enticed by footwear from Salvatore Ferragamo, Charles Jourdan, Chanel and Bruno Magli. *Open Mon.-Thurs. 10am-6pm, Fri. 10am-10pm, Sat. 9am-10pm, Sun. 11am-7pm.*

Clint Alan

212-869-8393

You loved the Ralph Lauren pumps, but you wish they didn't have an ankle strap and that you could walk at least one block in them without crying. Stop wishing and phone Clint Alan. Alan creates very sexy custom shoes with a unique padding system to reduce chafing and soreness without the Easy Spirit stigma. The best part: he'll come right to your apartment for a fitting and consultation if you can't make it to his showroom. Custom shoes start at $375. Shoes are ready in 1 to 3 weeks (rush orders can be done in as quick as 3 days if you're willing to pay). Also look for Clint Alan Collection of ready-to-wear shoes, ranging from Tod's-inspired moccasins to his trademark gold triangular stiletto heel, at his showroom and in fine stores around the city.

Cole Haan

667 Madison Ave. (at 61st St.) Upper East Side 212-421-8440

620 5th Ave. (at 50th St.) Midtown 212-765-9747

For those young Barbara Bush types, heels here tend towards the lower and wider, or the nonexistent. Find the classics like mules, riding boots, loafers and a couple of pumps. *Open Mon.-Sun. 10am-7pm.*

Hogan

134 Spring St. (near Wooster St.) SoHo 212-343-7905

Comfortable-chic occasions call for Hogan's snuggly shoes in staid designs. This Italian designer is now adding heels to the mix (which they promise will be comfy too). *Open Mon.-Sat. 11am-7pm, Sun. 12pm-6pm.*

Jimmy Choo

645 5th Ave. (at 51st St.) Midtown 212-593-0800

Although this diva shoe designer may be best known for his stiletto sandals adorned with real dia-
monds—namely a 22-carat momma dangling from the ankle, he does make teetering shoes for
mortals, too. You'll spend more, that's much more, than you should ever tell your
boyfriend/mother/boss about—but oh, is it worth it. *Open Mon.-Sat. 10am-6pm.*

Kerquelen

44 Greene St., (near Broome St.) SoHo 212-431-1771

430 W. Broadway (near Spring St.) SoHo 212-226-8313

Shelves and shelves of designer boots, kitten heels, stilettos, stack heels and flats from international designers like Dorotea and Jaime Masaro from Spain, Italian label Nina Hohendorf, and
bags to boot. *Open Mon.-Sat. 11am-8pm, Sun. 11am-7pm.*

Manolo Blahnik

31 W. 54th St., (near Fifth Ave.) Midtown 212-582-3007

You know the name, you know the deal—breathtakingly sexy shoes so popular that apparently
even muggers can recognize them. Think of them as an investment. *Open Mon.-Fri. 10:30am-
6pm, Sat. 10:30am-5:30pm.*

Otto Tootsi Plohound

38 E. 57th Street, (near Park Ave.) Midtown East 212-231-3199

413 W. Broadway, (near Spring St.) SoHo 212-925-8931

137 Fifth Avenue, (near 20th St.) Flatiron 212-460-8650

An arsenal of European brands, like Miu-Miu and Costume National, run the gamut from stilettos
to kitten heels to comfy flats. Don't overlook the house label footwear in the hottest styles at a
fraction of the designer label prices. *57th St. store open Mon.-Wed. 11:30am-7:30pm, Thurs.-Fri.
11am-8pm, Sat. 11am-7pm, Sun. 12pm-6pm. W. Broadway and 5th Ave. stores open Mon.-Fri.
11:30am-7:30pm, Sat. 11am-8pm, Sun. 12pm-7pm.*

Sigerson Morrison

28 Prince St. (between Elizabeth and Mott Sts.) NoLita 212-219-3893

Edgy shoes, with original embellishments like patterned insoles, beads, buckles, chains, topstitching, and bows. Find kitten heels, stilettos and lots of comfy, stylish flats. *Open Mon.-Sat. 11am-7pm, Sun. 12pm-6pm.*

Tod's

650 Madison Ave. (near 60th St.) Upper East Side 212-644-5945

Covers most of the style bases, from flats to semi-skinny heels, but you'll never walk in without seeing a tassel or two — conservatism is the key here. *Also see Handbags, page 197. Open Mon.-Sat. 10am-6pm (except Thurs. 10am-7pm), Sun. 12pm-5pm.*

CLOTHING

If there's one thing the Big Apple has no shortage of, it's clothing stores. If you can handle the madness of the department stores like Macy's, Bloomie's, Saks, Bendel's and Bergdorf's, you'll most likely walk out with something new and exciting for the evening. But, oftentimes, the best and most unique finds are housed in smaller boutiques in the East Village, SoHo and NoLita (see Shopping in NoLita, page 50). Scan Madison Ave. for designer wares and don't forget about cheapie stores like the Rainbow Shop, H&M and Joyce Leslie for those trendy pieces you'll most likely wear and toss. No matter where you live, there's always a Gap, Banana Republic, Express, Bebe, Zara and Club Monaco for last-minute reasonably-priced, if not predictable, fashion fixes.

Anna

150 3rd Avenue (btw. Aves. A and B) East Village 212-358-0195

Proprietor Kathy Kemp combines her unique creations (like sexy plunging dresses, cowl-neck tops, and "the essential suit" in corduroy or pinstripe; $50-$200) with a selection of vintage wares. *Open Mon.-Fri. 1pm-8pm.*

Anna Sui

113 Greene St. (btw. Prince and Spring Sts.) SoHo 212-941-8406

Sui's characteristically colorful rock-sweet gear always makes a bold statement. *Open Mon.-Sat. 11:30am-7pm, Sun. 11:30am-6:30pm.*

Barneys New York

660 Madison Ave. (at 61st St.) Upper East Side 212-826-8900

236 W. 18th St. (near 7th Ave.) Chelsea 212-826-8900

Where the ladies who lunch meet the ladies who max out their credit cards, all with a common goal—to find the most sought-after clothing around. What can you say about Barneys? Walking through those doors is as close as I've ever come to a religious experience. The Co-op store (at 18th St.) doesn't stock the Prada and Gucci, but offers names of mega-allure like Katayone Adeli,

Theory, Seven and Diane Von Furstenburg, along with accessories and a selection of beauty lines. Uptown is where the big names live. Both Madison Ave. and 18th St. *Locations open Mon.-Fri. 11am-8pm, Sat. 11am-7pm, Sun. 11am-6pm.*

Diane Von Furstenburg

385 W. 12th St. (btw. Washington and West Sts.)

West Village 646-486-4800

Along with those signature wrap dresses, DVF designs feminine, affordable tops, slim pants, and lots of LBD's and breezy skirts in her characteristic brights, patterns and as of late—a barrage of black, too. At her flagship shop, you'll also find shoes by the wrap-queen herself and Christian Louboutin, as well as handbags, both bearing the DVF label, and by international designers. *Open Mon.-Fri. 11am-7pm (except Thurs. 11am-8pm), Sat. 11am-6pm, Sun. 12pm-5pm.*

Fab 208 NYC

77 E. 7th St. (btw. 1st and 2nd Aves.) East Village 212-673-7581

Designer Jo Smith turns out unique, downtown, reasonably-priced clothing (shirts hover between $25-49; nothing over $100). Next door, shop for vintage accessories and clothing—a collection currently inspired by Pat Benatar and Chrissy Hind. *Open Wed.-Sun. 12pm-7:45pm.*

Fiorucci

622 Broadway (at Houston St.) SoHo 212-982-8844

That heavenly pair of angels has made a major comeback. The Italian clothing kingpin of yore is back and ready to dress you for your evenings on the town. Choose from the house-label stock or a mix of other European designer collections you'll be hard-pressed to find elsewhere. *Open Mon.-Sat. 11am-8pm, Sun. 11am-7pm.*

Intermix

1033 Madison Avenue, (near 77th St.) Upper East Side 212-249-7858
125 Fifth Avenue, near 19th Street Flatiron 212-533-9720

A one-stop shop for designer clothing, purses, shoes and accessories, Intermix has a finger on the fashion pulse. Look for: Marc by Marc Jacobs, Tocca, Theory, Tracey Feith, DVF and smaller labels high on style. House label creates great incarnations of the current trends. *Madison Ave. open Mon.-Sat. 10am-7pm, Sun. 12pm-6pm, 5th Ave. open Mon.-Sat. 11am-8pm, Sun. 12pm-6pm.*

Jeffrey

449 W. 14th St. (near 10th Ave.) West Village 212-206-1272

This store caters to the rich and richer, but everyone's got to splurge once in a while, right? Sometimes quality outweighs quantity, so stop in to explore the racks of high fashion from all of the Seventh Avenue and European stars. Shoes and accessories are all here too. *Open Mon.-Fri. 10am-8pm (except Thurs. 10am-9pm), Sat. 10am-7pm, Sun. 12:30pm-6pm.*

Lucky Brand Dungarees

38 Greene St. (near Grand St.) SoHo 212-625-0707

172 5th Ave (at 22nd St. and 5th) Flatiron 917-606-1418

216 Columbus (at 70th St.) Upper West Side 212-579-1760

There's just something about a garment that's actually printed with the word "lucky." How can you go wrong with great-fitting denim in lots of styles? *Greene St. shop open Mon.-Sun. 11am-7pm, 5th Ave. open Mon.-Fri. 10am-8pm, Sat. 11am-7pm, Sun. 11am-6pm. Columbus Ave. open Mon.-Sat. 11am-8pm, Sun. 12pm-7pm.*

Marc by Marc Jacobs

403 Bleecker (btw. W. 11th and Bank Sts.) West Village 212-924-0026

Stop wishing those perfectly-faded vintage Levi's just had a lower waist and a better fit—Jacobs knows exactly what you want, which is why his downtown nouveau-vintage look is one of the world's current favorites. His bridge line Marc by Marc Jacobs is more affordable, if not a bit of a worthwhile splurge, functional and whimsical too. Marc Jacobs Collection accessories are also available. *Open Mon.-Sat. 12pm-8pm, Sun. 12pm-7pm.*

Marc Jacobs

163 Mercer St. (near Houston St.) SoHo 212-343-1490

The designer who brought downtown chic to Seventh Avenue offers that fabulous vintage flavor, cut with a modern silhouette. This outpost sells pieces from the Marc Jacobs Collection, as well as his bags and shoes. *Open Mon.-Sat. 11am-7pm, Sun. 12pm-6pm.*

Mavi

510 Broome St. (at W. Broadway) SoHo 212-625-9458

Dark denim is a requisite part of the seasonless urban uniform. Nobody does the slim, hipster jean (available in a variety of lengths) quite like Mavi. Sift through the vintage selection (you might get lucky), and check out the denim and corduroy jackets (S54-S78). *Open Mon.-Sun. 11am-8pm.*

Mayle

252 Elizabeth St. (near Prince St.) NoLita 212-625-0406

Retro style with a distinctly modern flair — lots of lace and prints for girly-girl moods. *Open Mon.-Sat. 12pm-7pm, Sun. 12pm-6pm.*

M Shop

177 Orchard St. (near Houston St.) Lower East Side 212-505-9371

Nothing is worse than putting in heavy prep time only to run into your outfit twin. Avoid duplication with duds by up-and-comers who show their designs here. Purchasing from soon-to-be-bigs means reasonable prices for seriously stylish, unique clothing. Purses, shoes and belts also sold. *Open Mon.-Sun. 12pm-8pm.*

Patricia Field

10 E. 8th St. (near 5th Ave.) Greenwich Village 212-254-1699

If you're hitting the club scene, Patty Field's is a must for hard-to-miss silhouettes in even harder-to-miss shades. All the accoutrements for drag queens and feather-hearted females are also available — glitter, boas, and even wigs are yours for the picking. *Open Mon.-Fri. 12pm-8pm, Sat. 12pm-9pm, Sun. 12pm-8pm.*

Rainbow Shop

450 Park Ave. S. (at 31st St.) Murray Hill 212-684-4849
320 W. 57th St. (btw. 8th and 9th Aves.) Midtown West 212-333-5490
20 Vesey St. (btw. Broadway and Church St.) Lower Manhattan
212-406-6044

For trends that won't make it to the next week, much less the next season, bring a $50 to the Rainbow Shop and you'll have a whole new wardrobe. Don't expect quality, but do expect to find lots of cute tanks, skirts and even denim that runs the gamut from designer knock-offs to hoochie-in-training. Call for other locations. *Park Ave. S. open Mon.-Fri. 9am-7pm, Sat. 11am-6pm, W. 57th St. open Mon.-Sat. 9am-7pm, Sun. 9am-5pm, Vesey St. open Mon.-Wed. 8:30am-6pm, Thurs.-Fri 8:30am-7pm, Sat 11am-5pm.*

Roberto Cavalli

711 Madison Ave. (at 63rd St.) Upper East Side 212-755-7722

If the occasion calls for over-the-top garb, it's got to be Roberto Cavalli. His star-studded clientele shines just as brightly as his ubiquitous boldly embellished denim. Expect to pay about $400 for a pair. Also stocked here are leather jackets and pants, lingerie and razor-sharp stilettos. *Open Mon.-Wed. and. Fri.-Sat. 10am-6pm, Thurs. 10am-7pm, Sun. 12pm-5pm.*

Scoop

1275 Third Ave (near 73rd St.) Upper East Side 212-535-5577

532 Broadway (near Spring St.) SoHo 212-925-2886

A multi-label boutique housing the likes of Earl Jeans, Dolce and Gabanna, and Petit Bateau. Fashionistas know that proprietor Stefanie Greenfield stocks shelves with the right stuff. Uptown location has taken over four stores to house all of its merchandise. There you'll find more clothing and accessories to choose from, along with shoes by Jimmy Choo, D&G, and Michael Kors, as well as the "Scoop It Up" outlet section where last season's duds bear slashed price tags. *Third Ave. shop open Mon.-Fri. 11am-8pm, Sat. 11am-7pm, Sun. 12pm-6pm. Broadway open Mon.-Sat. 11am-8pm, Sun. 11am-7pm.*

Square One

32 E. 14th St. (btw. 5th Ave. and University Pl.)

West Village 212-229-0487

Sometimes all you've got is a spare $20, but you just can't bear to wear the same old thing. Forgo your fashion prejudice and realize that cheap is also good. Mixed in with the ostentatious club wear and over-done translations of runway looks, you'll find great tanks, tees and jeans that give higher end lines a run for their money. *Open Mon.-Wed. 10am-8pm, Thurs.-Sat. 10am-8:30pm, Sun. 10:30am-7:30pm.*

HANDBAGS

Looking for that special sling? That killer clutch? Perhaps a mini-baguette is what you crave. Most designer boutiques and clothing shops offer a selection of purses (don't miss DKNY, Scoop, Intermix and Barneys), and all of the major department stores sell the prestige brands along with more affordable items. When you love the designer look, but won't pay the price, you can always hit Chinatown or the various vendors on Lexington outside Bloomie's and all around the city— just remember that when you're making an appearance on the chichi scene, a fake Fendi can, and will, be spotted a mile away—you're better off with a unique bag or even a vintage model that has a style all its own.

Amy Chan

247 Mulberry St. (btw. Prince and Spring Sts.) NoLita 212-966-3417

Here, you'll find Amy Chan's signature mosaic tile bags, covered in eye-catching acetate chips in a multitude of styles and colors. Recently, leather and fabric bags have been added to the selections, along with lots of urban apparel like Frankie B's famous low-riders, Submission's feminine commando denim and L.A.'s Alicia Lawhorn collection. *Open Mon.-Sun 12pm-7pm.*

Anya Hindmarch

29 E. 60th St. (near Madison Ave.) Upper East Side 212-750-3974

For women of the mind that a bag is an investment, Brit designer Hindmarch will ensure that yours is significantly more stylish than your 401K plan (especially these days). From retro pop art-inspired designs (like chewing gum appliqués) to sophisticated leather models to beaded evening bags, the variety is rich. Some models even have coordinating shoes for the matchy-matchy minded. *Open Mon.-Sat. 10am-7pm.*

Blue Bag

266 Elizabeth St. (near Houston St.) NoLita 212-966-8566

A smattering of internationally designed bags in all styles and shapes. *Open Mon.-Sun. 11am-7pm.*

Coach

620 5th Ave. (at 50th St.) Midtown 212-245-4148
For other locations, see www.coach.com

The recently revamped collection is now one of the hippest around. While the logo'd look is taking a back burner, lots of their buttery leathers in a range of hues are ripe for the picking. Take a look through the tiny slings, shoulder bags and larger tote styles. *Fifth Ave. shop open Mon.-Sat. 10am-8pm, Sun. 11am-6pm.*

Deco Jewels

131 Thompson Street (btw. Houston and Prince Sts.)

SoHo 212-253-1222

Trends aside, there are some bags that defy time. Lucite bags were made only from 1949-1959 in the US. At least a dozen companies crafted entire bags of the sparkly plastic for day and evening. At Deco Jewels, Janice Berkson stocks at least 250 Lucite bags by companies like Willardy, Charles Kahn, and Llewellyn. Expensive in their day, these collectible bags are now priced between $200 and $2000. *Open Mon.-Sat. 12pm-8pm, Sun. 12pm-7pm.*

Dooney & Bourke

20 E. 60th St. (btw. Madison and Park Aves.)

Upper East Side 212-223-7444

This 25-year-old label has millennium-ized itself with lots of new designs, footwear and a brand new flagship boutique. *Open Mon.-Sat. 10am-6pm.*

Kate Spade

454 Broome St. (at Mercer St.) SoHo 212-274-1991

The woman who revived the popularity of non-leather bags has expanded her material palate to include lots more than the manmade stuff. The designs embellished with that telltale tiny black label continue to hover in that understated-sleek range. *Open 11am-7pm Mon.-Sat., Sun. 12pm-6pm.*

Keni Valenti

212-967-7147 *By appointment only*

At his eponymous showroom, Valenti stocks over 10,000 vintage purses coveted by fashionisti and style-makers alike who know his keen eye for fashion prophesy is right on cue.

Lulu Guinness

394 Bleecker St. (btw. 11th and Perry Sts.) West Village 212-367-2120

Now Manhattanites have their very own slice of old-world London smack in the middle of SoHo. Lulu Guinness's newly-opened shop—an adorable space—sells her line of whimsical evening and day bags, from flower-topped silk pots to butterfly clutches. *Open Mon.-Sat. 12pm-8pm, Sun. 12pm-7pm.*

Roberto Vascon

140 W. 72nd St. (near Columbus Ave.)

Upper West Side 212-787-9050

If you can resist the allure of instant gratification, plan ahead (about 20 days) and head to this upper west side leather shop. Create your dream bag from an arsenal of 200 Italian leathers in a range of colors, patterns and finishes in Vascon's variety of shapes. Whether you've got the design bug, or lack the creative gene, Vascon will guide you through the design process in an enlightening, enjoyable way and then whip it up for you in-house ($50-$300). *Open Mon.-Sat. 11am-7pm Sun. 11am-6pm.*

Sigerson Morrison

242 Mott St. (between Prince and Spring Sts.) NoLita 212-941-5404

Now the footwear design duo does handbags (there is a God!), and in honor of the new collection, the former shoe store, has been transformed into a handbag shop to house their purses, totes, small leather goods and luggage. *Mon.-Sat. 11am-7pm, Sun. 12pm-6pm.*

Tod's

(see page 189 for contact information)

Modern classics: satchels, wristbags, evening bags, travel bags and sophisticated over-the-shoulder looks in buttery leathers.

LINGERIE

Whether you're planning to display your unmentionables, are aiming to prevent visible panty lines, or just like to look delectable through and through, what you wear underneath can be just as important to a gal as what's on top. All the fast-fashion houses like the Gap (now opening Gap Body stores about the city), Banana Republic, Express, and even Diesel sell lots of bras and panties in a smattering of styles. For whimsical designs check stores like Wet Seal, Joyce Leslie, and Urban Outfitters. Department stores sell all of the big names, from Calvin Klein to more traditional labels like Bally and Maidenform.

La Perla

777 Madison Ave. (btw. 66th and 67th Sts.)

Upper East Side 212-570-0050

A name that even men know as synonymous with sexy, tasteful lingerie. *Open Mon.-Sat. 10am-6pm.*

La Petite Coquette

51 University Pl. (btw. 9th and 10th Sts.) West Village 212-473-2478

All that's pretty and frilly and sexy can be found here. In-house label, as well as a selection of cultish French lingerie brands are available in this bi-level shop. *Open Mon.-Wed., Fri. and Sat. 11am-7pm, Thurs. 11am-8pm, Sun. 12pm-6pm.*

Orchard Corset Center

157 Orchard St. (btw. Rivington and Stanton Sts.)

Lower East Side 212-674-0786

Bought a second-skin dress that looks oh-so-perfect...except for that little poochie belly? Well, despite the fact that men actually love our little tummies, sometimes we don't. For temporary flattening, check out body shapers and girdles that do the job without the pain. You'll also find lots of specialty bras for full-figured women (the store stocks cup sizes up to J), and those hard-to-find bras for backless, strapless, or asymmetrical necklines. A serious fitting will ensure you buy the bra you really need. *Open Sun.-Thurs. 10am-6pm, Fri. 10am-3pm, closed Sat.*

Wolford

619 Madison Ave. (btw. 58th and 59th Sts.)

Midtown 212-688-4850

996 Madison Ave. (btw. 77th and 78th Sts.)

Upper West Side 212-327-1000

122 Greene St. (at Prince St.) SoHo 212-343-0808

The hosiery king also sells the extremely teeny "t-string," the built-in bra top, seamless models, transparent-strapped bras for tricky garments, and a variety of other bras and panties. *619 Madison Ave. location is open Mon.-Sat. 10am-6pm, closed Sun. 996 Madison Ave. open Mon.-Sat.10am-6pm, closed Sun. Greene St. open Mon.-Sat. 11am-7pm, Sun. 12pm-6pm.*

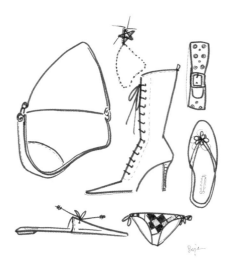

About the Author

Daniella Brodsky is an avid fan of both Miller Lite and the Cosmopolitan. While she spends a good portion of her nights bar-hopping (after primping, finding the right outfit and willing companions), by day she can be found playing guinea pig for the latest beauty treatments, gasping in awe at the newest fashions, researching current interior design trends, and talking to lots of interesting people about their lives for the various pieces she writes for magazines, newspapers and books. She is at work on her first novel.

Photo by Greg Mango

About the Illustrator

Sujean Rim has done freelance illustration for Barneys New York, *Elle Decor*, J. Crew, and the Clubmom.com. She has also completed several private commissions. Sujean enjoys fruit, fashion, and most everything mentioned in this book. Her inspiration comes from friends, Crazy Max, Mom, and Stink. She lives in New York City.